Publications of the
Institute of Germanic Studies
Volume 16

THREE ESSAYS ON THE
HILDEBRANDSLIED

THREE ESSAYS
ON THE
HILDEBRANDSLIED

by

FREDERICK NORMAN, O.B.E.

Late Professor of German, King's College, London
and Director of the Institute of Germanic Studies

reprinted and edited in honour
of his memory
on behalf of the Institute of Germanic Studies

by

A. T. HATTO, M.A.

Fellow of King's College, London

together with a letter by Andreas Heusler

INSTITUTE OF GERMANIC STUDIES
UNIVERSITY OF LONDON
1973

International Standard Book No. 0 85457 052 7

PRINTED BY W. S. MANEY AND SON LTD   LEEDS LS9 7DL   ENGLAND

CONTENTS

v

ACKNOWLEDGMENTS

I wish to thank the following for their invaluable assistance with this volume: Mrs Martha Norman, for lending me Andreas Heusler's letter to her late husband and allowing me to print it here; Professor Leonard Forster of the University of Cambridge, for agreeing to let me reprint his tribute to Frederick Norman, here reproduced from *The Times* by permission; Professor Peter Ganz of the University of Oxford, for help and encouragement in the early stages; Professor Emeritus William Robson-Scott, Honorary Director of the Institute, for his general supervision and advice; Maurice O'C. Walshe Esq., M.A., Deputy Director of the Institute and a fellow pupil of Norman's, for reading the proofs with me; V. J. Riley Esq., M.A., A.L.A., Librarian of the Institute, for his assistance in preparing the typescript for the press; and the Institute's Committee of Management and Publications Committee under the Chairmanship of Dr G. Templeman, M.A., F.S.A., for their unfailing support during this undertaking.

A. T. H.

FREDERICK NORMAN, O.B.E., M.A., F.S.A., was born in London on 23 November 1897. He was educated partly in Germany and during the 1914–1919 War he was interned at Ruhleben. After the War he studied at University College, London, where he held the post of Assistant, later Lecturer, in German from 1922 to 1930. Between 1926 and 1930 he also acted as Head of the Department of German at Reading University. In 1930 he was appointed Reader in Medieval German at King's College and University College, London, and in 1937 he succeeded to the Chair of German at King's College. From 1939 to 1945 he was attached to the Foreign Office, latterly as Liaison Officer to the Air Ministry, with the honorary rank of Wing-Commander. He served as a member of the Senate of the University of London from 1938 to 1966 and was Dean of the Faculty of Arts, University of London, from 1946 to 1950 and Dean of the Faculty of Arts, King's College, from 1946 to 1948. He held the post of Honorary Director of the Institute of Germanic Studies, University of London, from 1956 to 1965. He served as Deputy Vice-Chancellor, University of London, from 1962 to 1964.

On retirement from the Chair of German at King's College, London, in 1965 Professor Norman was appointed Academic Vice-President of the Institute of European Studies (Chicago). In 1966 he was appointed Mellon Professor, University of Pittsburgh. He was awarded the Gold Medal of the Goethe-Institut, Munich, in 1964 and a Prize as 'Leading Foreign Germanist' from the Deutsche Akademie für Sprache und Dichtung in 1965. Professor Norman died in Vienna on 8 December 1968.   W.D.R.S.

INTRODUCTION

Aʟʟ who have concerned themselves seriously with Germanic heroic poetry will know the name of Frederick Norman, and they will know it for the quality rather than the quantity of what he wrote. For throughout his career Norman felt a deep reluctance to commit himself in print. Prominent in his own account of this diffidence was the exasperating perfectionism which he attributed to his tutor Robert Priebsch, who time and again when Norman was ready to publish his M.A. thesis[1] recalled some out-of-the-way article affecting his study and asked him to incorporate it, so that (Norman maintained) the day came when a last straw from Priebsch broke the camel's back. Another reason for Norman's shyness of print was his acute awareness of how scholars raise monuments to their own folly, an awareness amply fed by generations of writers in his field. Here the scathing strictures of A. E. Housman at Norman's own college[2] were not without their effect. Following a hint from Mrs 'Dickie' Norman, however, I have come to see over the years that perhaps the overriding reason for the disproportion between Norman's wide and very varied knowledge and what he published was his intense absorption in other modes of living through speech, so that it seemed he had no 'Sitzfleisch' for writing articles and books. His amusing affectation that the entire business of medievalist scholarship is to edit and re-edit texts also worked for economy of output and is enshrined in his remark to a colleague, some twenty-five years gone: 'The

I

trouble with you, Mr X, is that you want to know what the texts *mean*'. Norman's edition of the Old English *Waldere* fragments[3] offers a fair example of what he judged the duties of a scholar and editor to be, and I have no doubt that the three essays on the *Hildebrandslied* reprinted here are to be regarded as prolegomena to an edition of the poem which, ours is the loss, it was not given to him to achieve.

The three essays were published when Norman was forty, sixty-one and sixty-six years old. The first is enlivened by the lingering zest of youth and by measured iconoclasm. A born rebel, Norman nevertheless knew where demolition should stop, proof of which is found in the warm response of Andreas Heusler to the gift of an offprint, appended below.[4] In his second, with what he called 'the débris of scholarship' cleared away, Norman was able to stand back and survey the text as guarantee of a once-existent whole, always with due regard to the wider poetic tradition. This was the work of his maturity, the outcome of much reflection during and long after the break of the war years. The third essay, which inevitably covers much the same ground, shows a change of mood no doubt occasioned in part by the change from English to German but also by the passage of a lustrum that brought him, ever-sensitive to his situation, within sight of retirement. From its beginning, despite the necessary digressions addressed to textual detail, this essay is somewhat vatic in tone, stating things with authority as though 'seen'. Norman's highly developed aesthetic faculty is here given freer rein both in the matters perceived and in the mode of their expression. It is interesting and perhaps significant that in order to gain this release Norman had recourse to his second tongue, of which he was such a master above all in speech, and an audience in a third, more distant land, albeit the land of his Ostrogoths and Langobards.

As a pupil of Norman's I had thought of digesting here all available publications on the *Hildebrandslied* subsequent to this third essay, but I abandoned the idea when it became clear to me how little real progress there has been. There is a notable exception however. Throughout his 'Zu Stil und Aufbau des Hildebrandsliedes',[5] Professor Ingo Reiffenstein of the University of Salzburg shows a warm appreciation of Norman's writings on the subject, and I am certain that Norman reciprocated this feeling with regard to Professor Reiffenstein's percipient contribution because of its close attention to matters of style and diction. The demonstration, calling on Old English, that the older 'epic vocubulary' was known to the late poet of the *Hildebrandslied* but that he chose to make a selective use of it for his own artistic purposes, must have delighted Norman, as, altogether, Professor Reiffenstein's assumption that the time has come to approach the great torso from the stylistic angle. As to the old bones of contention: Where do lines 46–8 belong? What brings the champions together between two armies — a divination as to which side will prevail? or a judicial combat? or both together? — in the present writer's opinion no progress has been made or ever will, for sheer lack of the means with which to conduct an argument. It is perfectly clear that lines 46–8 must be spoken by Hadubrand (otherwise we make Hildebrand the victim of sloppy self-pity to which he is a stranger) and it is equally clear on stylistic grounds that lines 46–8 are misplaced after

44 'tot ist Hiltibrant, Heribrantes suno!'

Even the editor of *c*. 800 saw that, since his misconceived *inquit* implies that he heard the finality of line 44 and thus the need to begin a new speech.[6] But *where* to place lines 46–8 nobody has shown.[7] As to J. de Vries's much-printed article on the plot of the 'father-slays-son' in its various manifestations in heroic narrative,[8] Norman at sixty-six seems to have been more tolerant than this pupil at sixty-two, since in Norman's final footnote to the third essay (the only footnote he allowed himself) he wrote: 'Mit vielen der von de Vries vorgebrachten Meinungen kann ich mich durchaus nicht befreunden, und ich werde mich in einem weiteren Aufsatz des näheren mit seinen Ansichten auseinandersetzen.' The choice of the words 'Meinungen' and 'Ansichten' instead of 'Argumenten' is significant. Norman had recognized that not a single argument based on evidence is offered to support any major aspect of de Vries's assertion that the 'father-slays-son' plot in the four Indo-European tongues descends from Indo-European myth.[9] Norman, then, was withholding his fire. Regrettably he never came to answering this article or to commenting on Professor Beyschlag's article[10] beyond his brief allusion in the same footnote.[11]

It was exciting and fascinating to be taught by Norman in his early thirties. Looking back and around, I am sure that in him I had the most wide-awake and universally stimulating tutor then alive who had anything to do with our subject. Perhaps only because of his geographical situation Andreas Heusler himself could not have introduced one, as Norman did, to such entrancing and profoundly significant entertainments as the classical Indian dance-drama or even to the Diaghilev ballet — for which Norman earned a season each year for himself and 'Dickie' Norman by marking German Matriculation scripts ambidextrously at the rate of thirteen an hour! I doubt whether there was any other teacher of medieval

German then alive who could have taken one through any half-opened door before which one happened to be standing and also some way along the road. So many doors and windows of his mind were full-open that it is remarkable that he achieved what he did in our narrow field. Thus it was for young people that Norman was at his best and most fruitful. I myself was doubly lucky to find him still young and gay with the gaiety of the post First World War generation, with an added relish from the brilliant internment camp at Ruhleben. Yet Norman was also apprehensive of the new war, which he foretold in my undergraduate days. Endowed with a good nose for such tricky matters as wine, racehorses and stocks-and-shares (as it later turned out), after his experience in the Oberprima of a Gymnasium in Hamburg he was particularly sensitive towards the possibilities of war: for of the thirty or so young German officers-to-be who had read Homer with him there until the summer of 1914, not one survived.

A factual obituary on Frederick Norman appeared in *The Times* newspaper on the 14 December 1968. His vivid yet elusive personality, however, had slipped through the net. It was to the delight of all who knew Norman that Professor Leonard Forster saw the need and under the date of 18 December supplied the tribute which, thanks to his generosity and that of the Editor of *The Times*, I am able to reprint here. Let this thumbnail sketch, for the accuracy of which many of Norman's friends and pupils can vouch, and of which Norman himself would have been the first to appreciate the sympathetic insight and literary skill, stand before and beside his three essays, effusions of his spirit on a subject very near his heart.

'May I add to your very factual obituary of Professor F. Norman? It conveys nothing of the vital and colourful personality of the man known characteristically throughout the academic profession as "Bimbo". Nomen est omen: the Italian word for a child in fact revealed something very deep in Norman. There is a sense in which he remained a small boy all his life. He preserved until the end the gusto, the quickness of wit, the intellectual curiosity of the formidably intelligent schoolboy that he must have been — and the immediacy and charm. These qualities gave life to his academic teaching and informed the influence he exerted on generations of students. His medium was the spoken, not the written word, in informal conversation rather than in the lecture room; his use of it was memorable. In this way he communicated in a uniquely personal manner his learning, enthusiasm, and the fruits of his wide-ranging, lightning-swift mind, and acted, in the words of your obituary notice, as a "Stimulator of German Studies".'

A. T. HATTO

Queen Mary College

London

August 1972

REFERENCES

[1] *Marienhimmelfahrt: ein mittelhochdeutsches Gedicht.* London, 1925. See the article based upon it: 'Notes on a Middle High German "Marien Himmelfahrt" ', *MLR*, 23 (1928), pp. 453–65.
[2] University College, London, where Housman had been Professor of Latin.
[3] London, 1933, in Methuen's Old English Library, of which Norman was co-editor with the late A. H. Smith.
[4] Pages 83 f.
[5] In: *Sprachkunst als Weltgestaltung*. Festschrift für Herbert Seidler. Hrsg. von A. Haslinger. Salzburg/München, 1966. Page 229 ff.
[6] The medieval editor's repetition of the half-verse 45b *heribrantes suno* from 44b in his invented 'inquit' is a gross offence to the ear. His mis-attribution of the speech to Hildebrand shows that the key to the old heroic style was already lost in the monasteries of the eighth to ninth centuries, a fact which need not surprise us. Similarly, the key to the shy native style of the Minnesang *c.* A.D. 1160 was lost within a few generations, to be fully recovered only in our own century.

⁷ S. Beyschlag (*Festgabe für L. L. Hammerich*. Copenhagen, 1962. Page 14 ff.) thought that lines 46–8 belong after line 57 on the grounds that 56–7, like 46–8, are concerned with Hildebrand's armour. But at 56 f., the reference to both suits of armour is a means of expressing the utter finality and irrevocability of the duel which Hildebrand now accepts; whereas the purport of 46 ff., is to throw doubt on Hildebrand's implied status as an exile. 46 ff., and 56 f., are incongruous as statement and counter-statement.

⁸ 'Das Motiv des Vater-Sohn-Kampfes im *Hildebrandslied*', printed for the third time with uncorrected mis-readings of the poem in *Zur germanisch-deutschen Heldensage*. Hrsg. von K. Hauck. Bad Homburg, 1961. Pages 248 ff.

⁹ See my article, which grew from my present duty, 'On the excellence of the *Hildebrandslied*. A comparative study in dynamics', *MLR*, 68 (October 1973).

¹⁰ See note 7, above.

¹¹ Page 82, below.

Some Problems of the *Hildebrandslied*

WHEN writing on the *Hildebrandslied* it has become customary to apologize for adding still further to the literature on the subject, and frequently commentators remark naively that it is difficult to find anything new to say, since every avenue has been thoroughly explored and every possible interpretation has been made (and rejected). The insistence on something 'new' is the bane of all true scholarship, and as most scholars in the Germanic field have considered it necessary to say something 'new' about the poem the literature on the subject is endless. Moreover, much of it has little value. When Steinmeyer wrote his commentary,[1] he singled out four contributions as 'völlig wertlos' and refused to consider them at all in his argument. Without detriment to the usefulness of his edition he could have left out at least forty. The notes in the latest edition of Braune's Reader[2] run to nearly thirteen pages, and most of the closely-printed matter is references to literature. Thus there are twenty-six different entries alone concerning the partially non-existent *wettu* in line 30, and the list is by no means exhaustive. Much of this accumulation of 'scholarship' might be consigned to everlasting oblivion.

There are some extenuating circumstances. The *Hildebrandslied* is the only early record of Germanic heroic poetry in the German language. It is fragmentary, and much of it defies certain interpretation. It is preserved in a dialect-mixture that could never have represented anything 'spoken', and even the character of the script shows a confusing medley of Carolingian, Insular and some Merovingian traits. The poem presents puzzles alike to palæographers, linguists and literary historians, and since on such debatable ground anything is tenable as long as it is supported by clever special pleading, [5/6] such wild and irresponsible guesses backed up by a great degree of learning and spurious scholarship are far more frequently met with than sane, cautious statement.

It is natural enough that linguists should have attempted again and again to solve the question of the dialect, but it is very unfortunate that so few of them ever remember they are dealing with a classic work of the heroic age and that, important as the linguistic implications and arguments may be, they are primarily not the concern of the literary historian. He is supposed to take linguistic criteria and conclusions into account, and he does. The linguist, however, pays scant regard on the whole to established literary facts, and is usually quite unaware of the literary absurdities that may be involved in his strict linguistic proof. One example will suffice, taken from F. Saran, *Das Hildebrandslied* (1915), otherwise an excellent commentary. Saran's conclusions are based partly on linguistic data, partly on evidence derived from Sievers's metrical theories.

Summarized, his theory runs: A Bavarian composed the poem round about 800 for a Saxon patron. He attempted, as well as he could, to compose in Old Saxon. Since he was not a very fluent Old Saxon scholar he produced the odd mixture of Old High German and Old Saxon which is still apparent in the extant text.[3] His poem was transmitted orally which led to omissions and corruptions. A second poet reconstructed the poem as best he could, and a cleric with grammatical training wrote down this reconstructed version. Of this last version our manuscript is a copy.

To begin with, the date 800 is demonstrably wrong. Clearly the *Hildebrandslied* is heroic court-poetry, in which case we have to assume an heroic poet and an heroic audience as necessary cultural background.[4] For these two essential pre- [6/7] requisites there is no evidence in Carolingian Germany. Otherwise it is a deliberately archaic production in the old heroic manner. This assumes a poet who was so well versed in departed traditions of heroic court-song that he made no mistakes in his heroic setting. It assumes further a patron with antiquarian interests. Unlikely as this may seem, it is far more probable than heroic composition in 800. 800 is an invention of linguists.[5] There is little to be said for it from a literary point of view.

The heroic code is presented simply and directly; wherever we are able to check the statements they give an accurate reflection of heroic times, and for general cultural and literary reasons we cannot assume that the poem was composed later than 700. If we wish we can postulate an original Gothic or Longobardic lay. The arguments for this are not convincing, and as long as we do not go later than 700 there is little to be said against original Bavarian composition.

The manuscript is certainly later than 800 though that in [7/8] itself proves nothing.[6] The *Beowulf* manuscript is late tenth century, but there is general agreement, outside the camp of Professor L. Schücking, that the poem, in all essentials in the form in which we have it, is not less than two and a half centuries earlier. The date 800 then, for the *Hildebrandslied*, is thoroughly unsound, and casts grave suspicions on the method of dating literature too exclusively on linguistic and metrical criteria.

Now for the poet. Even if we accept 800 as a feasible date we have to imagine a Bavarian poet, versed in antiquated heroic traditions and equipped with all the necessary stock-in-trade of heroic diction who is able and willing to compose partly in a foreign language. For by this time Bavarian and Old Saxon are sharply divided by the High German sound-shift, and it must have been much easier for Northern English monks to make themselves understood in Saxony than for Bavarians. We have to believe, therefore, in a true poet who treats of a grand and noble theme in a grand and noble manner but who presents his work in an uncouth gibberish that has no cultural reference and that must have struck listeners either as a monstrous parody or as a linguistic joke.[7] But even if we [8/9] accept this odd poet and his still odder audience we have to credit further the oral transmission of this newly created dialect from reciter to reciter. This would lead to corruptions, according to Saran, and that is the first piece of common sense in the whole elaborate construction. It may seem futile to argue over such unreal hypotheses, yet Saran was a scholar of some authority and his opinions have been widely commented on and discussed. The fantastic conclusions he arrived at were wrapped up in such a wealth of detailed and closely-reasoned linguistic and metrical criteria that many students, lulled into insensibility by an astonishing display of scholarship, blindly accepted statements that were palpably absurd.

The translation of linguistic facts into literary discussion is almost bound to lead to unacceptable conclusions unless due regard is paid to the literary side. It is possible that really valid linguistic proof could be adduced informing us that the *Hildebrandslied* was first committed to writing in a certain dialect at a certain time. That would necessarily mean that in a certain locality, at a certain time, there was an interest in such themes. This would form a proper and valuable starting-point for a close historical, cultural, and literary study of the region indicated. But such a linguistic proof could not and would not prove that the text was composed within these local and temporary limits, and much harm has been done by the failure to realize that linguistic facts must be confined to their proper realm. A good deal of the muddle-headedness apparent in discussions of the *Hildebrandslied* comes from neglect of this elementary rule.

If linguistic analysis has not been particularly helpful to the literary historian, let us see what it has been able to do in its own field. In more modern times only one scholar has tried to prove that the manuscript preserves a consistent dialect.[8] Usually it is realized that the manuscript confronts [9/10] us with a sad mixture of High German and Low German elements, and there are many features that point to particular High German or Low German regions. Assuming as a basis for argument that graphic peculiarities refereable to a particular region must have been contributed by somebody who had a hand somewhere in the transmission of the text, quite a number of permutations and combinations become possible. Most of them have been tried during the course of the last hundred years, and the theory of Holtzmann[9] (Low German copy of a Bavarian copy of a Franconian original) is by no means the most complicated. The battle over High German and Low German has now died down. For a long time it was curiously parochial, most North German scholars, beginning with Müllenhoff, asserting northern origin. The northern contingent was re-inforced by the Americans (Collitz, Karsten, Wilkens, Wood), some of the Scandinavians, R. C. Boer from Holland, and lately by Professor J. Mansion, who still inclines, in 1932, towards a northern origin.[10] Yet there is no further cause for argument. The Low German elements have been proved to be quite gross and superficial dialect-criteria like *t* for *ʒ*, and even, in some cases, non-existent *tt* for correct High German *ʒʒ*, whereas the High German traces are, on the whole, the subtler distinctions that appear, for instance, in flexional endings.[11] This proves High German origin on the linguistic plain as definitely as there is any need without troubling the literary arguments which pronounce overwhelmingly in favour of South Germany. Carefully used, these linguistic conclusions can give us some literary information. They prove that heroic material was still current — though they do not prove or disprove its composition — in Upper Germany in the eighth century in alliterative form, they prove further that there was some interest in Upper German song in more northern [10/11] regions. Much has been said about the way in which heroic lays travelled from tribe to tribe: here we have irrefutable evidence for the lay as it travels. Not that the linguistic form of the text represents a stage from South to North. It is quite impossible that the poem could ever have been recited in the form in which we have it. Steinmeyer's careful theory has most to recommend it. He says: 'Der Aufzeichner — who, from the general sense of Steinmeyer's argument, must have been an Upper German — hörte das hochdeutsche *Hildebrandslied* in einer niederdeutschen Gegend von einem Niederdeutschen vortragen und war nun bestrebt, die ganz besonders ihm auffallenden niederdeutschen Eigenheiten in seiner Niederschrift zu konservieren.' Steinmeyer, cautious to the last, puts this theory in the form of a question (op. cit., p. 13). His question, however, fits the facts more neatly than all other statements.

Saxon Germany is peculiarly deficient in early heroic material. Wayland the Smith was possibly Westphalian in origin,[12] there probably existed a Thuringian song of Iring, and that is almost all we know of. It is not, of course, essential that every Germanic tribe should have busied itself with the composition of heroic lays but the dearth of early heroic material is a little curious when one remembers the wealth of heroic fable among southern, western and northern neighbours. The Southerners had the Ostro-Gothic Theodoric material and the *Walter*-lay, the Franks must have developed the earliest *Sigfried*-lays and the story of the fall of the house of Gunther looked at from the Burgundian point of view. The Angles, as we know from English evidence extending deeply into the middle-ages, brought a good deal of heroic material with them to England, probably already in alliterative form. Perhaps the Saxon lays lacked wider appeal, and were thus forgotten. Even if we cannot [11/12] say much of early heroic literature in Saxony we know that in later times the Saxons were second to none in their interest in the old stories. They never took kindly to sophisticated French Arthurian romance, and continued to cultivate the old heroic material, though in a form more suitable to later days. Thus at the dawn of German literature proper we have the welcome evidence of Low German influence on the *Hildebrandslied*, and at the very end of the middle-ages we have a song reflecting the Harlungen tragedy. Jordanes, in the middle of the sixth century, gives one account (in chapter 24 of *De origine actibusque Getarum*); the Icelandic *Hamðismál* gives another version. Up to about the year 1000 there are frequent references though they are never sufficiently clear to give an accurate outline of the story. The interest dies down, everything seems forgotten, and then Low German produces a ballad round about 1560 on the death of Ermanaric. This late Low German ballad is not an unmixed blessing: it sets many more problems than it solves, but it does prove continuity of interest and tradition. One more example: the *Atlamál en grœnlenzku* knows of a son of Hagen the Niblung who helps Guðrún to slay Atli. The Greenland poet has invented a name for the son, Hniflungr; he also places him in rather different circumstances. Yet he knows the essential fact: Hagen's son revenges his father's death on Attila. This must be derived from a Low German lay though we have no knowledge of how the news travelled to the distant North. Finally, there is the vast biography of Theodoric, the *Þiðrikssaga*,[13] culled in the main from Low German material, and the accounts there given deserve rather more respect than Dr Perrett seems willing to concede.[14] It is not reasonable to expect a compilation made in the middle of the thirteenth century to present the same point of view as a poem going back to the heroic age. When all allowances have been made for later times and manners the *Þiðrikssaga* has much to report that is of interest, and in [12/13] one important passage it gives us a clue to the end of the old lay of Hildebrand that we cannot afford to neglect (see below, p. 21 [p. 24 and note 27]).

Dr Perrett starts with the old text and argues implicitly that the older version must be the more original one. It may be, though this is not a self-evident truth. Dr Perrett further rejects, and quite rightly, wanton interference with either the transmitted text or the plain and obvious meaning. This is a sounder method than the former one of reckless emendation. There is general agreement among students, if not among professional emenders, that emendation must stop, and it would be well to take stock of the position and to discover how much of value a century's re-writing of the text has produced. Most editors regularize *-brant* and *-braht*, printing the former, restore *w* where *p* and the *wynn*-rune have led to confusion, supply *h* before *r* or *w* in *ringa* 5, *wer* 8, *welihhes* 10/11, *werdar* 61 and delete the *h* in *gihueit* 18, *bihrahanen* 57, *hrumen* 61. The alliteration *hiutu: hregilo* 61 seems to prove the point[15] for an older stage of the poem, and if editors wish to show their phonological knowledge not much harm is done. It is, however, a pity to regularize since forms like *gihueit* 18 show that *h* before *r* or *w* was an orthographic symbol that stood for nothing in particular, an important fact for dating and localizing the manuscript which is less telling when relegated to the foot-notes. Of emendations proper the following are generally accepted: *mir* for MS. *min* 13b (Lachman: *mî*, von Grienberger *mîn'* = *mî nû*); *sid* for MS. *d& sid* 23a (*d&* is usually taken to have crept in on account of the following *detrihhe* but since the name is not spelt with the symbol *&*, some editors print *det sid* and have to admit that they do not know what it means); *fateres mines* for MS. *fatereres mines* 24a; *gistuontun* for MS. *gistuontum* 24b; *fehta* for MS. *feh&a* 27b; *inan* for MS. *man* 43 (*man*, nevertheless, makes sense). Apart from purely orthographical [13/14] matters, then, the manuscript has been altered in six places only, and four of these agreed alterations occur between 23a and 27b which include the mysterious repetition *darba gistontun* to which we shall have to return. So much for all the misplaced ingenuity of scholars who have attempted to re-write the lay!

Since this matter is of general importance let us consider the latest batch of alterations, proposed by that inveterate emender, Professor Axel Kock,[16] a scholar of such deserved repute that his suggestions are bound to creep into the apparatus of future editions, to the dismay of all those who try to keep abreast of this never-ending stream. There are four of them:

Lines 10/11 are usually printed as:

fireo in folche . . . . . .

. . . . . . '*eddo hwelihhes cnuosles du sis*'.

The alliteration is missing, the general sense is clear. Some editors print the statement as one long line. Now Kock suggests *fatercnuosles*.[17] This is certainly better than inventing a line, a procedure adopted by no less than ten well-known and respectable scholars! Yet there is nothing to be said for it. If a Germanic warrior asks another for his *cnuosl* he means: Who is your father? The Germanic tribes were patrilineal.[18] If we must interfere with the text it were better to write *kempheo in folche* which would alliterate and give good sense. Not: 'Who among the people in the army' but 'Who among the chosen champions in the army'. The substitution of *kempheo* could be argued at length and plausibly. However, it is *not* put forward as an emendation and let us hope it is kept out of the footnotes of future editions. If anybody [14/15] wishes to puzzle over these lines there is the real difficulty of the subjunctive *sis* in direct speech. About this nobody has bothered except von Grienberger[19] and Dr Perrett. The explanation of the former is forced and fanciful. A subjunctive in Old High German meant something, and the usage here cannot be paralleled. The corruption is not to be sought in the poet's mind but in the dilatoriness of a succession of copyists. Originally the statement was either *du bist* and the subjunctive was carried on mechanically from *wari* in line 9,[20] or indirect statement continued to the end of the line which must then have been *her si*.

The *du sis* must then have got in from '*ibu du . . .*' in line
12a. The best course is to leave the text as it stands, and
note the oddity, as Dr Perrett does.

Line 15 reads: *dat sagetun mi usere liuti.*

There is no alliteration, and there are many suggestions.
None is acceptable. Professor Kock now proposes *suderne
liuti*, and this is really inexcusable. Here we have the
emender not even bothering to look up the type of
literature that he is helping to increase. For *suðerliuti* was
suggested by Rieger in 1906[21] and by the brothers Grimm
in 1815,[22] almost at the beginning of the study of the text.
Now *usere* has the most emphatic position in the line,
first stress in second short line, and emenders should take
particular care before they remove a word from such a
prominent position. Hadubrand says: people of my own
kith and kin, i.e. trustworthy people. These people
are further described as 'aged and experienced'. Line
[15/16] 16b reads: *dea erhina warun* = who lived formerly,
i.e., who are all dead now. M. Trautmann[23] feared that
listeners might have understood Hadubrand to refer to
dead witnesses which would be 'zwecklos, um nicht zu
sagen unsinnig', and von Grienberger (op. cit., p. 29)
adds that it is quite irrelevant whether they are dead or
not at the time of the conversation between father and
son. 'Senseless' and 'irrelevant' are strong words to use
when discussing the work of an unknown poetic genius
whose fame has endured through the ages. Hadubrand
naturally prefers the testimony of his own countrymen,
and when Hildebrand announces that he is the long-lost
father and — from Hadubrand's point of view — tries to
put the younger man off his guard by fine words and
presents, Hadubrand must immediately think of two
things. The aged and experienced men on his own side

who knew Hildebrand are gone beyond recall. There is therefore nobody in his own country who could vouch for Hildebrand's statement. The younger man must further realize that the old Hun (*alter Hun*, line 39) is quite capable of putting two and two together and that he is perfectly safe in pretending to be Hadubrand's father. It has frequently struck editors that up to this point Hadubrand has been courtesy itself, and has been most willing and guileless in supplying personal information to his adversary. Since they could not account for the abrupt change of mood that follows editors have often dubbed the text 'corrupt' and imagined that a good deal has been omitted. We can get along perfectly without assuming omissions. Hildebrand's phrase, line 31, *sus sippan man*, can only mean 'I am your father', and that is the way Hadubrand and listeners understood it. There is no doubt whatever that this is what the poet expects his audience to grasp. And the beginning of Hildebrand's answer makes this still plainer. The original witnesses are all dead, and the old warrior calls upon the heavenly powers to bear witness for [16/17] him when he exclaims in line 30: *wettu*[24] *irmingot* (*quad Hiltibraht*) *obana ab hevane* ... Hildebrand, in his greatest need, calls upon the heavenly powers to avert the catastrophe; Hadubrand, his suspicions thoroughly roused by what follows after this appeal to the godhead, can only regard Hildebrand's mortal agony as dowright blasphemy and the perfidious attempt of an abject coward to gain his victory by a perjured oath to the Lord of all. Blasphemy, perjury, treacherous offer of gifts. No wonder that the hitherto courteous Hadubrand swings round completely, and that his next speech is a torrent of abuse. He calls Hildebrand an incredibly wily old Hun who is lulling him into a false sense of security in order to attack him, when he is off his guard, with a dastardly blow. The next line (41): *pist also gialtet man so du ewin inwit fuortos* is translated by Ehrismann: 'Du bist ein so alt gewordener Mann, wie Du immer Betrug ausgeführt hast'. This is neither German nor sense. The meaning is: Only by fighting unfairly on every occasion have you managed to grow so old. This final insult comes, appropriately enough, at the end of Hadubrand's tirade. He merely adds, as a fact to clinch the matter, that he has certain information from seafarers about the fate of his father: *tot ist Hiltibrant, Heribrantes suno* (line 44). Henceforth, Hadubrand remains silent, and we must agree with Dr Perrett, on the internal evidence of the lines discussed here (15 ff.) that lines 46–8 must belong to Hildebrand, as the text says they do (but cf. p. 7, note 5). Other and later sources cannot invalidate the internal evidence of the text itself. For Hildebrand there is no option. Son or no son, he must kill, if he can, any man who dare assert that his honourable fighting career was a fraud from beginning to end.

A consideration of Professor Kock's emendation of *usere* has of necessity led to other problems. That was inevitable; *usere* is a key-word, the poet knew what he was doing, and [17/18] *usere liuti* must not be touched. The line would normally alliterate on a vowel, and one would expect the alliteration to fall on the place occupied by the entirely neutral and colourless *sagetun*. As in the case of *fireo in folche*, discussed above, it is not intended to add to the conjectures; *antwurtun*, not suggested by the commentators who mostly confine their efforts to ruining the second short line, does no violence to the sense and solves the alliterative problem, if we wish to solve it.

Line 31 reads: *dat du neo dana halt mit sus sippan man.*

Again, there is no alliteration. Professor Kock wants *danasid.* This is not recorded in Old High German, and he therefore supports it by the Gothic *panaseips*. This alteration helps us no further, nor do all the others. The glossary to Braune's Reader supplies many words beginning with *s* that have not yet been tried.

Line 60: *gudea gimeinun: niuse de motti.*

This has been excellently defended by Dr Perrett. Professor Kock now alters *niuse* to *goume*, meaning 'take heed'. This is a great weakening of the sense of the transmitted text, and there is nothing to be said for it.

*   *   *

Of the two methods of treating a text, re-writing it or justifying it, Professor Kock prefers the former, Dr Perrett the latter. In one place of his article Dr Perrett follows the former method, not indeed by alteration of a word but by drastic re-arrangement. Lines 12 and 13 are transposed and *chind* assigned to the end of line 11. This does not disturb the manuscript position of *chind* in relation to the now following line but it produces an alliterative short line *du sis chind* with alliteration in an unusual place and an insufficient number of syllables. Dr Perrett has ably vindicated line 60 with its unusual alliteration. When an extremely rare metrical form occurs in a text [18/19] we may not be able to do anything about it but we cannot construct lines that show such a rare form. Leaving out other evidence and confining ourselves exclusively to the *Hildebrandslied* we find that of 58 alliterative lines, 56 have alliteration on the first lift of the second short line, and only two on the second lift (lines 51 and 60). This is doubtful evidence for introducing such rarities. Dr Perrett's new line also has so-called 'unterepische Füllung'. This is extremely rare in West-Germanic verse, and the few examples found are all suspect. If we meet with them in a text we may have to leave them; they cannot be regarded as safe models. Furthermore, transposition of lines 12 and 13 seems unnecessary; it makes line 12 appear as a disconnected after-thought, whereas, as the text stands in the manuscript, line 13 is a well-linked general statement summarizing the reasons for the enquiry. We shall have to leave the text as it stands, though not without misgiving. There is, as Dr Perrett convincingly shows, something radically wrong with *chind*.

Lines 23 ff.: *sid Detrihhe darba gistuontun*
fateres mines: dat was so friuntlaos man.
her was Otachre ummet tirri,
degano dechisto unti Deotrichhe darba gistontun.
her was eo folches at ente, imo was eo fehta ti leop:

We have already noted above that four of the six generally agreed alterations of the text occur in this short extract of five out of sixty-eight lines. In additon, *tirri* is gravely suspect, *dechisto* can only be explained by postulating an otherwise unknown West-Germanic adjective corresponding to Old Norse *þekkr*, and that only if *þekkr* is etymologically divorced from the root in 'think', an unconvincing demonstration. There seems little doubt that this section is peculiarly faulty in transmission, and such considerations do not allow us to regard the four words *unti Deotrichhe darba gistontun* too complacently. Moreover, variation is the soul of Germanic [19/20] verse, not repetition. Most editors print *miti Deotrichhe*, and banish the rest. This is feasible palæographically. J. Grimm took *unti* as 'apart from'. There is no certain evidence to show whether *unti* could bear that meaning. The statement would not have been unbecoming. From

late migration times onwards Theodoric had become the
Bavarian national hero, and it is praise indeed for a
warrior to be considered the next best man to Theodoric.

Dr Perrett is the first scholar who has put up a strong
case for the retention of the whole of the manuscript
reading. He plausibly connects *darba gistontun* with the
tragic fate that overtook Theodoric's retainers, largely
through the fault of Hildebrand, towards the end of the
Nibelungenlied. He may be right, but if he is we shall have
to re-write large sections of the theory of the gradual
development of the epic. The postulated Bavarian lay of
the fall of the Niblungs would assume quite different
proportions, and the authority of the *Þiðrikssaga* as a
valuable guide in the re-construction of lost lay and epic
material would be undermined. Dr Perrett has raised an
interesting problem, and we shall have to go far afield in
order to realize fully all that is implied.

The *Hildebrandslied* contains (a) the story of a fight
between father and son, (b) various allusions to Theodoric
and his long exile. Let us deal with (a) first. Fights between
father and son, with either tragic or happy ending, are
known the whole world over. Potter[25] collected a great
number and many more have been adduced since. The
poet had either heard a similar story or he invented it
himself. Commentators are agreed that the father slew the
son,[26] and significant hints for [20/21] the reconstruction
of the end of the lay are found in later versions.[27] We may
deduce: The father overcomes the son, and thus vindicates
his honour. He is willing to spare his life. Hadubrand,
lying defeated on the ground, aims a treacherous blow at
the unsuspecting old man who is leaning over him. A
bitter irony of fate when we recall the flaming indictment
of cowardly behaviour that has fallen from the defeated
warrior's lips only a short while before. Hadubrand's

taunts thus receive added significance. Thereupon Hildebrand kills him. Better an only son dead than a living coward!

The father-son conflict concerns two people only: Hildebrand and Hadubrand. There is mention of Heribrand, the father of Hildebrand, and of Hildebrand's wife who remains nameless. Hadubrand in later tradition is Alebrand. The same story, with happy ending, is told again and again;[28] Alebrand, either the same person or the same name, appears in a number of other contexts in later heroic poetry. Yet he never has a role assigned to him and remains little more than a name. This can only mean that he was specially created in order to be killed by his father. Heribrand, later Herbrand, also occurs, but again as a mere shadow and relation, usually father, of [21/22] Hildebrand. He also seems to owe his existence to the *Hildebrandslied*. The mother is later on given the name Ute, and variants of this. She receives father and son when they return together after the recognition scene. She also is occasionally mentioned though she has no context outside the father-son story. She is another invention of the unknown original poet. There remains Hildebrand.

Müllenhoff suggested the Goth Gensimund as the historical prototype of Hildebrand. According to Cassiodorus, Gensimund was the faithful companion of the royal brothers Valamir, Vidimir and Theodimir, and was praised in song for his constancy and loyalty. The suggestion has been often repeated. However, we may prefer the caustic comment of Professor Schneider: 'Der Name stimmt nicht, eine Fabel oder Rolle, die sich fortgeerbt hätte, besteht nicht, die Funktion ist ganz typisch — welchen Wert hat also der Hinweis auf Gensimund'?[29] We cannot escape the surmise that Hildebrand was probably invented by the poet himself.

To obtain more evidence on this point, however, we have to examine his connexion with Theodoric.

This is more easily said than done. The evidence concerning the development of the Theodoric figure is conflicting in the extreme. In the case of the Niblungs we have early historical information tolerably well preserved, though shifted to a personal rather than a political plane; we have the wealth of lay-material in the Edda and the *Vǫlsungasaga* which supplies some of the Eddic gaps of the *Codex Regius*. Unfortunately, Theodoric seems to have reached the North rather late, at a time when the general heroic outlines had already become fixed, and there is nothing in Iceland that can help us. There must have been a Theodoric-epic in Germany before the end of the twelfth century. The hints we have do not suffice to build up a consistent story, let alone consistent details. In the case of the Niblungs a great poet arose shortly after [22/23] 1200 who welded together traditions and produced the *Nibelungenlied*. Theodoric, the favourite Upper German hero, became an important figure in this epic but no great poet honoured him in the way in which the Niblungs had been honoured. At the close of the classical period, between 1250 and 1300, Theodoric epics began to appear. Now it was too late, and now the poets produced too many. There are preserved eleven complete epics and the fragments of two more, all recounting stories of Theodoric and his heroes. There is far too much material and it is well-nigh impossible to sift the earlier accounts from later accretions. Broadly speaking, there are two types of story connected with the Gothic king, (a) heroic adventures in normal human setting, (b) stories of battles with dragons, dwarfs, giants and other disreputable folk. The latter must be later than the former. The earliest story under (a) would appear to have been connected with

Theodoric's flight from Verona (Bern) and his exile of thirty years. The time-limit of the exile presupposes the eventual return. The Old English *Deor* knows he returned since he is cited as an example of misfortune outlived. Our earliest authority for the flight and exile is the *Hildebrandslied*, which means that the poet of the *Hildebrandslied* knew one or more Theodoric-lays. The *Hildebrandslied* knows: On account of the enmity of Odoaker, Theodoric fled towards the East. With him went Hildebrand and many of his warriors.[30] Hildebrand was a great stand-by to Theodoric. They lived at the court of Attila the Hun.[31] Hildebrand returned with a Hunnish army after thirty years. These facts would not have detained an heroic poet for more than a few lines. They are not the outlines of a plot, they are the merest background. Where is the essential heroic fable? In later accounts [23/24] Theodoric is always victorious, yet he always flees! The later versions know that Theodoric was victorious but that eight of his companions were taken prisoner. He redeems them by giving up his empire. Some scholars have argued that this motive solves the riddle and supplies our plot. This is quite unlikely. The story seems to be the invention of a later poet who was as non-plussed as we are. In an early heroic lay the hero would have hacked his way through to his companions and freed them, or would have perished in the attempt. This would have given a powerful lay on the old theme: loyalty of prince and retainer, but with fighting instead of weak though noble submission.

Theodoric's return to his ancestral realm is just as mysterious. Ermanaric dies and Theodoric rides home! On the return journey Hildebrand has his fight with Alebrand (*Þiðrikssaga*). The *Hildebrandslied* has a different back-ground. Two chosen champions meet between the armies drawn up for battle. Here the return does not seem to be quite so peaceful. More we cannot state.

Unlike his relations, Hildebrand is a clearly-defined figure who occurs again and again as an active participant in other events. But as far as the evidence goes he does not appear to be connected with Theodoric until later times. The earliest companions seem to have been Wittich and Heime, the Old English Widia and Hama, and we are doing no violence to the facts if we suppose that the poet invented Hildebrand and connected him with the famous Theodoric. The *Hildebrandslied* makes Hildebrand leave and return with the king, thus giving the former thirty years' fighting exile. Here was a gap that might be filled. We know that the *Hildebrandslied* was recited for centuries, and there was thus ample opportunity for new creations with the Theodoric-Hildebrand pair.

Dr Perrett would like to connect *Hildebrandslied* and *Nibelungenlied*. If we are to believe the *Þiðrikssaga*, compiled round about 1250 but depending, in this particular instance, on [24/25] the older *Nibelunge not*, written about 1160, this cannot be.[32] In the *Nibelunge not* it is Theodoric who rushes in with Hildebrand and all his men to avenge the death of Roðingeirr[33] (*Nibelungenlied*: Rüedeger), just as it is Theodoric who kills Kriemhild. For the last poet Theodoric is 'a verray parfit gentil knight', and both these episodes are handed over to the more heroic and less courtly Hildebrand.

There must have been current in Bavaria, well before 800, a lay of the fall of the Niblungs. In this lay Kriemhild had ceased to kill her husband Attila in revenge for the slaying of her brothers (Frankish, anti-Hunnish tradition), and killed Gunther and Hagen in revenge for the slaying of her first husband Sigfried. Bavaria had no use for a treacherous Attila. Theodoric was known to be at Attila's court, and already in this poem it must have been Theodoric who overcame the Niblungs when the Hunnish warriors failed. On the Niblung side there can have been at most four champions. Are we to believe that the Bavarians would have tolerated a lay in which this handful of imported champions defeated the companions of Theodoric, the chief Bavarian hero? The Bavarian fall of the Niblungs cannot have been on so large a scale, nor is there room in a lay for an important minor plot. That is the business of an epic.

The up-shot of all this is as unsatisfactory as ever. The second *darba gistontun* refuses to be explained. We shall have to admit regretfully that the text seems to be corrupt here, and we shall have to leave it at that. There is one thing, however, that we can say, and it is the only thing that really matters. [25/26] The language of the lay is an intolerable mixture, there are probably some gaps, some words and phrases we are unable to interpret, many lines are clearly corrupt since they do not alliterate, the end is missing. Yet we give our thanks across the ages to the Fulda monks who, tutored in the preservation of heroic remains by their Anglo-Saxon brethren, did their best to save the poem from utter destruction, for in spite of all draw-backs we can still realize and appreciate the essential beauty of the poet's conception, and in these sixty-eight lines a poetic genius is revealed to us whose terse work need not fear comparison with the great tragedies of literature.

[Reprinted from London Mediæval Studies. Edited by R. W. Chambers, F. Norman, and A. H. Smith, 1 (1937), pp. 5–26.]

REFERENCES

[1] E. von Steinmeyer, *Die kleineren althochdeutschen Sprachdenkmäler* (1916), 11.

[2] W. Braune, *Althochdeutsches Lesebuch* (ninth edition, edited by K. Helm, 1928).

[3] Saran nails his colours to the mast when he states (p. 77): 'Daraus folgt, dasz die bunte Sprachform des HL. mindestens in allem wesentlichen ursprünglich ist, also dem Dichter I zugeschrieben werden musz; Dichter II hat sich bei seinen Stücken streng daran gehalten.'

[4] One essential difference between a modern and a mediæval poet is frequently overlooked. A modern poet may, if he chooses, disregard his readers completely. A mediæval poet is socially bound. He creates for an audience whose code he accepts and whose aspirations he expresses. The further we go back in mediæval days the stricter the social control becomes.

[5] The weightiest piece of linguistic evidence occurs in line 48. There, *riche* alliterates with *reccheo* from **wrakjo*. The time-value of the evidence for the dropping of initial *w* before *r* and *l* in Bavarian is difficult to assess. J. Schatz, *Altbairische Grammatik* (1907), 94 (§88c), says: 'Vor *r, l* ist anlautendes *w* schon im 8. Jahrh. nicht mehr vorhanden.' Since our earliest Bavarian documents take us back to not later than 750, and since scribal practice lags behind speech-development, we could assume that the sonorous quality of *w* before *r* was not of much account by 700. G. Baesecke, *Der deutsche Abrogans und die Herkunft des deutschen Schrifttums* (1930), argues that *wr* was current in Bavaria later than is usually granted. Realizing the force of the literary arguments he quotes A. Heusler's surmise that the *Hildebrandslied* might be Longobard in origin, connects this with surviving Gothic families in the Longobardic realm, and envisages the possibility that the *Hildebrandslied* could have been transliterated from Gothic into Bavarian after 785 (p. 158 f.). This is ingenious but leaves us where we were before. Such a Gothic poem of earlier date is unlikely to have alliterated *r : wr*. This would mean that line 48, in its present form, might have been supplied later, and the moment we admit that, the evidence against earlier Bavarian origin falls to the ground. In any case, all is not well with lines 46–8. That line 46 shows no alliteration is a minor blemish. A greater difficulty is the sense of the lines. Even if they express bitter irony they do not really fit in with what goes before and what follows. The only proper reply to Hadubrand's insolence, culminating in the taunt of line 41 (see below, p. 17 [p. 20, above]) is line 49: *welaga nu, waltant got (quad Hiltibrant), wewurt skihit.*

[6] There is one point in connexion with the manuscript that has not received the attention it merits. For *w*, both scribes employ the Anglo-Saxon *wynn*-rune, though not consistently. Both place a long acute accent over the rune, though again not always. Avoidance of possible confusion with *p* is the obvious reason. Now is this an idiosyncrasy? If not, where else does this accent occur? As far as we know it is never found in English manuscripts though there it would have been still more useful on account of the added possibility of confusion with the *thorn*-rune. In Germany, the *wynn*-rune also occurs, without accent, in the Trier fragments of the Salic Law. Here the letter is a poor, illiterate specimen (cf. the reproduction in G. Könnecke, *Bilderatlas zur Geschichte der deutschen Literatur* (2nd ed., 1912), 9), valuable merely as showing that good Anglo-Saxon scribal tradition stood behind the scribes of the *Hildebrandslied*. Does the rune, accent or no accent, occur in any other German manuscript?

There is a cultural side to this which can hardly be exaggerated. Anglo-Saxon Christianity showed great common sense and commendable leniency in its dealings with vernacular heroic poetry. It is significant that the only remaining piece of early German heroic verse should have been written down in the Anglo-Saxon foundation Fulda and that the manuscript should show unmistakable signs of Anglo-Saxon scribal influence.

[7] We are not offended by the language of the *Hildebrandslied* since our appreciation is reconstructed and intellectual, not immediate and emotional. A parallel will help. What would our reactions be if Shakespeare had intended Hamlet's speeches to be delivered in an inconsistent mixture of Scottish and Somerset forms?

[8] F. Kluge, *Hildebrandslied, Ludwigslied und Merseburger Zaubersprüche* (1919), argued for Middle-Franconian. Nobody accepts this.

[9] *Germania*, ix. 289 ff.

[10] J. Mansion, *Althochdeutsches Lesebuch* (2nd ed., 1932), 113 f.

[11] The evidence is excellently assembled and interpreted, as long as the interpretation remains linguistic, in Saran's commentary.

[12] It must be admitted that this is a little doubtful. The postulated connexion with classical fables becomes more difficult the further the tribe is situated from Roman spheres of influence. On the other hand, the hero Wittich was thought to be the son of Wayland already in the eighth century, and *Þiðrikssaga*, based largely on Low German material, is very partial to Wittich.

[13] *Þiðriks saga af Bern*, udgivet . . . ved Henrik Bertelsen, 2 vols., 1905–11.

[14] 'On the Hildebrandslied,' *MLR*, xxxi, 532–38.

[15] *ringa: hiltiu,* line 5, the proof usually cited, is not a proof at all, for in that line the alliteration may well be *helidos: hiltiu*.

[16] 'Zum Hildebrandslied,' *Zeitschrift für deutsches Altertum*, LXXIII, 47 ff.

[17] The emendation is supported by a reference to the Old English *fædrencnosl*. We are not told that the word occurs only in the Laws of Alfred in a technical context where great precision is required: *be ðæs fædrencnosles were* = 'according to the weregild of the father's kin.'

[18] In this connexion it is worthy of note that the five male characters referred to in the lay are named. Attila is circumlocuted as *Huneo truhtin* which, to a Germanic warrior, could only mean Attila. But the only woman mentioned remains nameless.

[19] Th. von Grienberger, *Das Hildebrandslied* (1908), 24: 'Dagegen gibt sich der zweite Fragesatz in 10 *eddo . . . du sis* entweder als Zitat einer von einem Dritten gestellten Frage, der auch Hildebrand selbst sein könnte, wenn er von sich in der dritten Person spräche, etwa "Hildebrand frägt dich," oder als Teil einer unmittelbaren Anrede, abhängig von einem nicht dastehenden Imperativ "sag" mir'.' An involved explanation follows.

[20] Such a slip could occur easily since no device is employed to mark off speeches.

[21] *Zeitschrift für deutsches Altertum*, XLVIII, 3.

[22] *Altdeutsche Wälder*, herausgegeben durch die Brüder Grimm, 3 vols., 1813–15. In II, p. 102 (the article is signed by J., i.e. Jacob, the elder brother) we read: *'dat sagetun mi usere sundro liuti*, oder *sudarliuti*, da Hadebrand in Süden wohnte, Hildebrand aus Osten kam.'

[23] *Finn und Hildebrand* (Bonner Beiträge zur Anglistik 7, 1903), 87. In this book Trautmann set out to prove that the *Hildebrandslied* was a translation from Old English. The book has at most a curiosity value. It is not worth reading.

[24] Treatment with reagents has practically destroyed this word, but the general sense is clear.

[25] M. A. Potter, *Sohrab and Rustem* (1902). The *Hildebrandslied* and its versions are discussed pp. 64–9.

[26] O. Rank, *Das Inzest-Motiv in Dichtung und Sage* (1912), 175 f., concludes that originally the son killed the father. 'Derjenige von den Gegnern, welcher mit inneren Zweifeln in den Kampf zieht, wird nicht seine gesamte Energie im Streit verwerten können und musz also eher fallen; im Hildebrand-Lied wäre der Sieg des Vaters gleichbedeutend mit dem bewuszten Mord des erkannten Sohnes und darum hat gerade der Ausgang dieses Zweikampfes so mannigfache Modifikationen erfahren.' The gruesomeness of the Germanic tragedy lies precisely in

the fact that the father, in spite of his abhorrence, *must* overcome any paternal weakness. Rank's analysis is correct but his conclusions are those of a modern writer, not of a Germanic poet.

[27] *Þiðrikssaga* (Bertelsen, II, 350). Alebrand is wounded, offers to submit. He makes as if to hand his sword over to Hildebrand. The latter puts down his shield and attempts to seize the sword. Alebrand attempts to hack off his father's hand. Quickly, the old man raised his shield, and said: *þetta slagh mun þier kient hafa þin kona enn æigi þinn fader* (Your wife must have taught you this blow, not your father). He thereupon defeats the son and forgives him. The last line of verse 10 of *Das jüngere Hildebrandslied* (critical edition by Steinmeyer in the third edition of Müllenhoff-Scherer, *Denkmäler deutscher Poesie und Prosa*, II, 26 ff.) runs: 'nun sag, du vile junger, den streich lert dich ein wip.' Here the blow is not dishonourable. All the poet permits himself to say is: 'Ich weiss nicht wie der junge dem alten gab ein schlag'. . . The cowardice has gone, there is now no point in the reference to a woman's methods of fighting. But it was a traditional line, and it was effective, so it was allowed to remain.

[28] Der Marner (13th century) knows a poem (K. Bartsch, *Meisterlieder der Kolmarer Handschrift*, Bibliothek des litterarischen Vereins in Stuttgart 58, 1862, 426, no. xciv) *von des jungen albrandes tot*. 'Alphartes' has been suggested as a correction, and Bartsch prints 'Ecken.' Neither is necessary. The poet probably knew a version which preserved the old, tragic ending.

[29] H. Schneider, *Germanische Heldensage*, I (1928), 317.

[30] It is not quite certain whether the warriors referred to (line 19: *enti sinero degano filu*) belong to Theodoric or to Odoaker. The poem could easily have been recited in such a way that no uncertainty could have arisen in the minds of the listeners. One does not understand why he ran away if he had so many friends. Cf. John Meier, 'Zum Hildebrandslied,' *Hermaea*, xxxi (*Strauch Festschrift*), 1932, 45 ff.

[31] This fact is not expressly stated, but it is a reasonable inference.

[32] This poem is not preserved though there is no question that it existed. We can re-construct it from the *Þiðrikssaga* and the *Nibelungenlied* which left much of it standing unaltered. And where the *Nibelungenlied has* altered it it is usually possible to prove why.

[33] *Þiðrikssaga* (Bertelsen, II, 321). Now King Thidrek saw that margrave Rodingeir was dead. He cried out: Now my best friend is dead. Now I can no longer remain inactive. Let all my men take up their weapons. Now I must fight with the Niflungs. Now Thidrek went down to the street, and it is said in German songs (*er sagt i þydeskum kuedum*) that it was not comfortable for cowards when Thidrek and the Niflungs came together in battle.

II

Hildebrand and Hadubrand

PART from purely antiquarian interest there was
never any reason why Germanic heroic literature
should have been preserved in written form at all.
The heroic song was not book literature, and we cannot
imagine a chieftain sitting down at the high seat, and
having an heroic poem read to him. It would therefore be
unfortunate, though not in the least surprising, if
Germanic heroic literature had survived solely in the form
of allusions and in occasional re-telling embedded in
chronicles and similar works.

Actually we have been more fortunate. England was
converted to Christianity when native tradition was still
strong and whilst Anglian Christian bookish literature —
even *Beowulf, Deor, Waldere* and *Widsith*! — is certainly
not Germanic heroic poetry it preserves form, vocabulary
and much of the outlook and ethos of earlier times. It also
presents us with scraps of story with which we must do
the best we can. In Iceland the conversion came far later;
on the other hand, heroic traditions survived far longer,
and christianized Iceland of the thirteenth century was
able to supply a rich harvest. Much could obviously have
been gathered in the Germany of the eighth and ninth
centuries, for later times provide abundant evidence for a
strong, indigenous literature. Yet there was a different
spirit abroad and little direct material has been handed on

to us. It is easy to blame the Church, though it is not very accurate to do so. The Church was certainly hostile to heathen tradition and heathen poetry; it was merely indifferent as far as heroic poetry was concerned. There was also an element of bad luck. We have no reason to doubt the information that Charlemagne caused a large collection of traditional poetic material to be made. That is an antiquarian practice which we can parallel in England and Iceland. We do not know whether this collection perished through the bigotry of his son and successor Louis the Pious. The 'carmina gentilia' which this prince liked in his youth and despised later on in life were classical Latin poetry and there is thus no evidence at all that he ordered the destruction of the Carolingian corpus of native verse. Probably, like so many other things, it just vanished through neglect and lack of any real interest.

And yet the different spirit in the Frankish realm must have had a good deal to do with the decay of native tradition as well. Throughout two centuries England produced many thousands of lines of alliterative verse devoted to Christian topics, but in Carolingian Germany Otfrid resolutely turned to rhymed verse, though in his own way he was proud enough of his Frankish native tradition. His chapter *Cur scriptor hunc librum theotisce* [325/326] *dictaverit*, after praising Greek and Latin writers for the formal purity and excellence of their style, nevertheless takes up the challenge, and attempts to emulate them in Frankish which, according to Otfrid, is as good a language as Greek and Latin in which to praise the Creator poetically. The lover of Germanic poetry may deplore the attitude of Otfrid and his deliberate unwillingness to follow in the footsteps of his Anglican brethren, he may wax indignant at his halting verse, and his rhymes may seem primitive and barbarous to him. But when all is said and done Otfrid is the one who is looking forward, he is making literary history, he is an innovator not an antiquarian, and the future lies with him and his kind. His importance for the development of German poetic technique can scarcely be exaggerated.

There was no epic in the grand manner in Frankish Germany before Otfrid. In Saxony there was. The *Heliand*, undoubtedly deeply influenced by Old English religious epic technique and yet in many ways going beyond it, is about forty years older than the *Evangelienharmonie*, and it is written in the old manner. Even if the poet of the *Heliand* was not educated at Fulda, and for all we know he may have been, he is much indebted to this English foundation and to the writings of its great teacher and abbot Hrabanus Maurus. Of Otfrid we know that he received a good deal of his education at Fulda. He has himself testified to this and to the influence which Hrabanus Maurus had on him. Fulda, as befitted an English foundation, was far less averse to encouraging native traditions. Later on in life when Otfrid was himself teaching further west and nearer to West-Frankish influences, he turned to poetic composition in the vernacular at the request, so he tells us, of good friends and a pious matron. But as far as he was able he broke with his Germanic background, and he wrote rhymed verse.

Writing was entirely the business of monks, and Otfrid's success killed alliterative technique in Germany. A few stray fragments may be post-Otfridian. They are not important. End-rhyme had won the day. In England, on the contrary, alliterative verse, for so long so actively encouraged by the Church, had such a secure hold that in spite of the vast influence of French models it could still be employed ambitiously and in his own way powerfully in the fourteenth century by William Langland. And there is still alliterative poetry on the Battle of Flodden.

Over 30,000 lines of Old English alliterative verse written before the Norman conquest have been preserved, by far the largest part having been carefully and beautifully written in magnificent codices specially devoted to this purpose. In Old High German we have a bare two hundred lines, and most of them in a shocking state of preservation.

Only two truly heroic fragments have been preserved in southern Germania. One is the Old English *Battle of Finnsburg*, the manuscript of which is now lost. Its linguistic forms suggest an eleventh-century date. The other is [326/327] the *Hildebrandslied*, part of the manuscript of which is also lost, at least for the time being. This was written down at Fulda at the very beginning of the ninth century. It is by far the oldest fragment of heroic poetry in any Germanic language. The writing shows marked insular characteristics and there is no doubt that the scribes were strongly influenced by English traditions. This fragment has unfortunately been transmitted in a linguistic form much of which cannot possibly represent any real language at all. Not only do we find Upper German and Low German forms side by side, we come across impossible dialect mixtures even in words. Thus there could never have existed a form such as *chud* — written twice in this odd manner — with its very Upper German aspirated *k*, its long Low German vowel due to loss of nasal and compensatory lengthening and its final High German dental. The monstrous *chud* is by no means an isolated example, though it is one of the worst. All this is commonplace, and agreed to by nearly everybody.

There is far less agreement on the manner in which this remarkable mixture could have arisen, nor does it seem very likely that any solution could be proposed which would satisfy everybody. Few would care to argue, nowadays, that the poem was originally northern and had travelled south, and there is thus substantial agreement on a High German origin of the immediate forerunner of our manuscript text. A purely linguistic analysis will take us no further than this Bavarian text of the second half of the eighth century, and here we are at once on debated ground, for some still maintain that this Bavarian version did not exist in manuscript form, and that the text was written down from memory, whilst at the same time an attempt was made to introduce Low German forms. Such a view poses more problems than it is able to solve.

There were two scribes. The second wrote ten lines only and then handed over again to his rather less expert colleague. There is almost universal agreement that the scribes left off where they did as there was no more room. This is not strictly speaking so. A good deal more could have been squeezed in. Unless, therefore, we wish to assume that there was some sort of interruption and that the labour was never resumed, it is far more likely that the text from which a copy was being made was itself fragmentary.

It seems that in one case we can actually prove careless copying. The two words *darba gistuontun* were written twice by mistake; *darba* occurs as *darba* on both occasions. This is a matter of some moment, to which reference will recur below. But *gistuontun* occurs both as *gistuontum* and as *gistontun*! And within eight consecutive lines Theodoric is given as *theotrihhe* (19), *detrihhe* (23), *deotrichhe* (26), and what is presumably the first syllable of the name — and an error — before the *sid* of line 23 as *dĕ*. The spelling of proper names is no fair test; nevertheless, the scribes do not inspire us with confidence. [327/328]

There are gross errors, obvious lacunae, misplaced lines, serious lapses against the alliterative canon, some lines which read like prose, and many minor blemishes; yet this fragment with its stark poetic economy remains one of the most remarkable productions of the heroic temper, ageless in its severe, uncompromising beauty and breath-taking in its rapid movement and its intense drama.

From other, later parallels we are familiar with the end. The father killed the son. We cannot reconstruct the exact manner in which the death of the son was brought about. The unknown poet dealt so freely with the inherited father-son story that it would be unwarranted to argue from the related versions in Ireland, Persia and Russia; and the later German accounts preserved in the *Thidrekssaga* and the *Jüngeres Hildebrandslied* give no clear line. Much has been made of the cowardly blow said to have been struck by Hadubrand. There is some evidence for this in the *Thidrekssaga* and in the statement in the *Jüngeres Hildebrandslied* by the old warrior: '*den slac lert dich ein wip*'. Yet both the *Thidrekssaga* and the *Jüngeres Hildebrandslied* are influenced by courtly literature and courtly ideals of literature round about the year 1200, and we must beware of arguing that originally Hadubrand was killed on account of some 'treacherous' blow. Yet some sort of trickery or cunning exists in the other versions. In the Irish account Cuchullin kills his son Conla with a terrible and a treacherous weapon after he has been defeated ignominiously at sword-play, at wrestling, and has been twice ducked in the sea during a swimming contest. Conla exclaims: 'my mother did not teach me about this weapon'. This is a curious parallel to the remark made in the *Jüngeres Hildebrandslied*. There is

HILDEBRAND AND HADUBRAND 39

not enough evidence to enable us to regard the remarks
as anything more than strange coincidence. In the Persian
version it is again the father who escapes death by a trick
when he is completely at the mercy of his son. Only in the
Russian variant is there any suspicion of foul play by the
son, who aims a lance at his sleeping father. The blow is
warded off by a cross which the father wears on his chest;
he jumps up and promptly kills his son. This Russian
story is, however, extremely late, it has all sorts of
accretions, and it cannot be regarded as a reliable guide.
We must therefore beware of drawing hasty conclusions.
'Rather a dead son than a living coward' is a modern
fantasy developed from the unreal conditions of late
medieval chivalry.

The *Hildebrandslied* is undoubtedly an heroic poem. It
is not, however, a typical one. In all other heroic poems
there is a plot in which the chief actors are involved.
Revenge for a wrong done, blood-feud, love of gold,
disputed inheritance: these are the commonest motives.
Almost invariably relatives are pitted against one another
and the breaking of blood-ties is a matter of course. In
this the *Hildebrandslied* conforms to the general pattern,
though here father and son have no quarrel. There is no
personal reason for [328/329] the fight, and where there is
no personal incentive — which would, of course, include
personal loyalty to the chief — there can normally be no
clash of a nature to interest the heroic poet. In the
Hildebrandslied the heroes either just happen to meet,
which seems to be largely the situation at the back of the
accounts in the *Thidrekssaga* and the *Jüngeres Hildebrandslied,*
or the heroes are chosen to decide, by the combat, the
issue of the battle. An analysis of the beginning of the
poem itself proves that we are here dealing with the latter.
It is an occasion when both the fighters are taking very

4

special care, and several lines are devoted to telling us how son and father prepared their equipment, got ready their armour, girded on their swords over the armour, and then rode out to the battle. We are thus dealing with a pre-arranged and carefully prepared single combat of picked champions, with both armies looking on. These champions were also presumably the leaders of the invading and defending armies, or they could be regarded as the chief representatives of Theodoric and Odoaker. The armies themselves remain completely static; they are never again mentioned. Yet we must not forget that they are there, silent, watchful, hearing and weighing every word that is spoken. All this we are able to gather from the poem itself, which assumes far less knowledge on the part of the hearers than is normal in heroic poetry. The poem is not, in fact, highly allusive; everything is most carefully explained except the reason why the two armies were there at all. Even that unfolds itself gradually by implication, and it would presumably have been completely obvious by the end of the poem.

The poem is therefore complete in itself; it is not an episode belonging to a wider context of both Hildebrand and Hadubrand. Everything that we know or need know of these two for a thorough understanding is contained in the text.

Nevertheless, the poet builds his plot into the Theodoric exile-story and he therefore assumes that his hearers have some knowledge of Theodoric and Attila. And here we are very much in the dark. However famous Theodoric was to become later on, and however much we may know about the historical Theodoric, we cannot construct a satisfactory heroic story which deals with the manner in which he left his realm and the manner in which he returned.

The victorious return of Theodoric to his kingdom after an enforced exile of thirty years should have been a warlike affair with stirring adventure and coherent plot. It is nothing of the sort. Similarly, the motivation of his exile never builds up into a reasonable and consistent story. The very first thing that we hear about this great hero is that he fled from his adversary Odoaker. Heroes do not flee, at least they do not flee in heroic poetry. Hundreds of years later excellent reasons are adduced for this flight: it was a self-imposed exile, undertaken in order to save his imprisoned companions. Such [329/330] generous behaviour is wholly intelligible later on in the Middle Ages, yet it would not seem to fit into the context of earlier heroic society. If your companions are imprisoned you rescue them, sword in hand, or you perish in the attempt.

The *Hildebrandslied* supplies the earliest evidence for the exile-story. There is not, however, sufficient evidence to construct a satisfactory plot. All we hear is that Theodoric fled from the hatred of Odoaker. And if we take the text at its face-value this flight involved not a solitary hero but also Hildebrand and many of Theodoric's thanes. A whole troop that fled? The text says so, unequivocally, and we must accept it. And at least one of the troop left his wife and young child at the tender mercy of the enemy! That, however, must be the invention of our poet.

And there we come to the heart of the matter. This poet did not bind himself slavishly to tradition. He knew the father-son story and its tragic outcome, and he re-arranged their story until it suited his purpose. In all other versions the son went abroad to seek the father, who had left a token which the mother was to give to him before he started out. Here it is the other way round, and there is no doubt that this is a deliberate construction by our poet.

He supplied names for his pair which had up till then not been heard in Germanic poetry: Hildebrand and Hadubrand. He even supplied an ancestor Heribrand. The last-named exists merely as the father of Hildebrand in the song itself; Hadubrand never acquires any sort of context outside this one story; but Hildebrand, the tragic father, became immediately famous, and he was very soon inseparably attached to Theodoric. He therefore began to share in the various adventures of Theodoric, and he was even pulled in to some of them which may have existed at the time the *Hildebrandslied* was created. That, however, does not prove that Hildebrand existed before the *Hildebrandslied*: it merely proves that he just could not be left out. Once this is realized many difficulties vanish.

A few years ago Elisabeth Karg-Gasterstädt published an article[1] on the difficult phrase at *Hildebrandslied*, 23 f.: *sid Detrihhe darba gistuontun fateres* [MS.: *fatereres!*] *mines*. It had always been assumed that this either meant: 'needs arose to Theodoric of my father', i.e. 'my father was useful to, helped Theodoric', or: 'absences arose to Theodoric of my father', i.e. 'Theodoric had to do without my father'. Nearly all editors have rejected the second interpretation, as Theodoric and Hildebrand were companions in arms and were invariably together. Elisabeth Karg-Gasterstädt, who had the advantage of the extensive collection of material for the *Althochdeutsches Wörterbuch*, was able to prove conclusively that *darba* in Old High German invariably had the sense of 'privatio', the opposite of *haba*: 'possession', and that therefore it always meant 'non-possession', 'Beraubtsein einer bestimmten Eigenschaft, die dem Subject im normalen Zustand zukommt'. Twenty [330/331] references to Notker's usage are given. Similar meanings are proved for *tharben*, *githarben*, *tharbon*, and the weak masculine *tharbo*: 'einer der an etwas Mangel leidet, etwas nicht hat, entbehrt'. The *Essen Evangeliar* supplies the adjective *tharfag*: 'Mangel, Entbehrung leidend' and in the phrase *tharfag uuerðan* as a translation for 'indigere' we have a very close parallel to *darba gistuontun*. There is a certain amount of 'Schadenfreude' in the conclusion:

Welcher Art die Trennung war, durch die Dietrich seines Waffenmeisters verlustig ging, mögen die Sagengeschichtler ausfindig machen. Mir scheint die Auffassung Francks, Hadubrand spiele auf den Tod seines Vaters an, sehr einleuchtend, doch könnte der Plural *darba* auch auf wiederholte Trennungen deuten, deren Ursache dann doch wohl selbständige Kriegsfahrten Hildebrands — vgl. etwa Hadubrands *her was eo folches at ente* oder sein eigenes *dar man mih eo scerita in folc sceotantero* — gewesen sein dürften.

There is little doubt that the interpretation proposed by Franck over fifty years ago is the right one. There were certainly no 'selbständige Kriegsfahrten' at the time the lay was composed.

Two speeches in the text are assigned to Hadubrand. The first one is fifteen lines long, and takes us from line 15 to line 31. The second speech begins at line 37 and ends at line 44. It is, however, probable that lines 46–8 which the manuscript assigns to Hildebrand, have been transposed, and that they in reality belong to the second speech of Hadubrand. That would make Hadubrand's second speech eleven lines.

The first speech is cunningly devised in such a way that it gives the father the necessary information for claiming that he is, in fact, Hildebrand. There are no witnesses who could identify Hildebrand, for the old and wise people who told the young man of his father are all said to be dead (*dea erhina warun*). These dead witnesses reported that the father's name was Hildebrand, and we should note the 'was'. It is the first indication of the son's conviction, which nothing can shake, that his father is dead. There follows the account of where the father went, why he went, and in whose company. As the text stands it is difficult to construct the sense in any other way than to refer *enti sinero degano filu*: 'and many of his warriors' to Theodoric, though it would be far better if these warriors could belong to Odoaker. It would explain, among other things, why Theodoric was so friendless (line 24). The older man is next informed that Hildebrand left behind a young wife and a young child, and that the two were entirely without protection or property. Then comes the statement, discussed above: 'later on Theodoric had to manage without my father.[2] He was a man without a friend.' The speech ends with the proud praise of the warlike qualities of the father, who was invariably in the thick of the fight, and who had a high reputation amongst brave men. The final summing-up: 'I do not imagine he is still alive' is polite, but in the context it can mean nothing else than 'my father is dead'. The fate of such [331/332] an outstanding fighting man, who was held in such renown by other warriors, could not possibly have remained unknown.

So far the younger man has remained courteous, forthcoming and obviously without guile or suspicion. He has presented the older man with all the information. The latter has nothing he could add, and there is no token that could help in the recognition. All he can give is his word. Commentators mostly assume that there is a gap here between the son's and the father's speech. There would appear to be a word or two missing from the son's last line which, moreover, lacks alliteration (*ni waniu ih iu lib habbe*). Nothing very much can be missing. The speech ends tellingly with the polite surmise of the father's death.

The older man's answer, as transmitted, is short. It is also, as far as its details are concerned, obscure. The exact interpretation of *wettu* — if that is what the manuscript originally read — is doubtful, though *irmingot* is clear enough. The next line looks very much like a prose paraphrase, and then there follows a half-line. Something is clearly very wrong though the general sense would not seem to have been seriously impaired. The meaning must be that the father calls upon God[3] to witness that Hadubrand has never had dealings with a closer relation (*sus sippan man*). It is said that the statement must follow that he is the long-lost father. Why? Hadubrand quite clearly has no other male relative, and in the context *sus sippan man* can only mean: 'I am your father.' Hildebrand follows up this avowal by the offer of golden gifts as a token of his goodwill.

This is too much for the formerly courteous Hadubrand. The reference to God must strike him as blasphemy, and from his point of view he quite rightly suspects a trap. His second speech is, therefore, of a very different calibre. Gifts made by enemies should be proffered on the point of a spear, not by hand. 'You are a cunning old Hun.[4] Whilst you are using fair words you are only waiting for a chance to throw your spear at me. You have grown old in wily practices.'

It is here that lines 46–8, assigned in the manuscript to Hildebrand, probably belong. In Hildebrand's mouth they do not really make very good sense; in Hadubrand's they are apt. Not that all is well with them. The first reads like prose and it has no alliteration, the third alliterates *riche*: *reccheo* which is not possible in Bavarian before about 750. They are, however, good lines, and the thoughts expressed somehow ring true so that one would like to claim them for the original in some form or other: *wela gisihu ih in dinem hrustim   dat du habes heme herron goten,   dat du noh bi desemo riche reccheo ni wurti*: 'it is perfectly obvious from your armour that you have a generous lord at home. You were never outlawed from this country.'

And then follows what is to Hadubrand's mind proof positive that the old man is lying: 'seafarers who came west over the Mediterranean reported to [332/333] me that he had been killed in battle. Hildebrand, the son of Heribrand, is dead.' Just as Hadubrand's first speech ends with the statement that his father is dead, although politely phrased, so the second speech again ends with the death of the father, but now it is a hard, factual statement that brooks no contradiction, and after the offer of gifts, and the contemptuous way in which they have been refused, there is no mistaking the scorn with which the information is being conveyed to the older adversary.

There is therefore no need to postulate any further lacuna. 'Woe now, almighty God, a terrible fate is about to happen' is a perfectly intelligible statement after Hadubrand's firm and final announcement that his father is dead. Nor is there any need to assume that Hadubrand once more intervenes before Hildebrand exclaims: 'Let him be the most cowardly (*argosto*) Easterner . . .', the argument being that just before Hadubrand must have called the old man *arg*! This is quite unnecessary. Hadubrand's second speech contains sufficient invective to justify Hildebrand's outburst.

After Hildebrand's last speech the fight is joined, and already after 5½ lines the warriors have arrived at a stage where the shields have been hacked to pieces. Clearly this poet is not going to waste overmuch time on the mere technicalities of the fighting. How he would have proceeded we cannot possibly tell except for the fact that

the son died and the father survived. The other versions
cannot help for this poet is so independent and so
supremely in charge of his story that it would be idle to
postulate any detail.

It may be permissible to draw some tentative con-
clusions. When this poet composed his lay there were
stories current concerning Theodoric and his exile with
Attila. The exile-story is early, though in the nature of
things it cannot have originated until a good while after
the death of the historical Theodoric (525). We cannot
assume a developed exile-story — whatever the motiva-
tion and plot may have been — until well after the middle
of the century, and by that time the Goths had lost their
hold on Italy and had been supplanted by the Langobards.
There is no doubt that Gothic traditions were taken over
and further developed by their successors, who then
handed them on to other tribes further north. How much
of this Gothic material was current in Langobard lays at
Langobard courts we cannot say. There is no convincing
reason why we should not assume that the whole of the
Gothic — and later — Theodoric material passed through
Langobard versions. As far as the *Hildebrandslied* is
concerned we are on tolerably sure ground. Names in
-brand, as Heusler first pointed out, are overwhelmingly
Langobard, and since his day sufficient evidence has been
produced to make Langobard origin very likely. This
would fit in well with the geographical details. The home
army is defending itself against invaders who are
streaming in from the Hungarian plains, and we may
assume that the two armies are encamped somewhere
north of a line running from Bern (Verona) to [333/334]
Raben (Ravenna). It therefore makes good geographical
sense that Hadubrand receives news of his father's death
from sailors who cross the Adriatic in a westerly direction.

Such completely correct details are unlikely to occur unless the poet is familiar with the district. They are mentioned in the poem as a matter of course, they fit in with what we know of the position of 'Bern' and 'Raben', and these details must have been familiar to the first listeners as well.

As for the date: the poem could have been current at a Langobard court any time after 600. It must have been produced well before 700 and it then made its way north into Bavaria. In Germany, 'der alte Waffenmeister' became almost a national figure, in England he remained completely unknown.[5] Somehow he travelled to Scandinavia, and this is remarkable, for the heroes of later southern lays, i.e. lays later than the first half of the sixth century, are normally unknown in the north. Yet the *Asmundarsaga kappabana* contains some verses, undoubtedly far older than the fourteenth-century saga, in which the dying Hildebrand, felled by his half-brother Asmund, describes his shield. This shield has pictures on it of the fighters whom he has overcome. There are said to be eighty! One of them is his own son, *enn svási sonr*, from which we cannot dissociate *suasat chind* of the *Hildebrandslied*.

The very obscurity of the Hildebrand figure in earlier days is a great help to us. The evidence before us is only intelligible if we assume that a Germanic heroic poet, probably a Langobard of the seventh century who knew the tragic father-son story, invented Hildebrand and Hadubrand, and then placed them in a context connected with Theodoric.

REFERENCES

[1] Elisabeth Karg-Gasterstädt, 'Darba gistuontun', Paul & Braune's *Beiträge*, vol. 67 (1945), 357 ff.

[2] *Fateres mines* is an odd and weak line in so early a poem and the manuscript reading *fatereres* does not increase our confidence. The reading *fater eres mines*: 'formerly my father' was suggested almost a hundred years ago. Whilst this does not interfere with the transmitted text, would give us the older genitive *fater* which we expect, and would make excellent sense, the construction is harsh and probably impossible. The adverbial genitive *eres* from *er* = 'formerly' could be compared with *eiris* in the first Merseburg charm. But although *eiris* for *eres* is not awkward syntactically, many have preferred to read *eines* = 'einst'. No solution can be suggested.

[3] We have to assume that author and audience were Christians. There is no 'heathen' spirit in this poem, as has been so frequently asserted. A tough fighter need not be a heathen, and a reference to cruel Fate is not unknown among devout Christians. The Langobards were Christians when they invaded Italy in the middle of the sixth century, though whether they were very pious Christians is another matter. Gregory the Great thought they were a thoroughly detestable crowd.

[4] 'Old Hun' is not of course meant as an insult. It is a purely factual description.

[5] Unless a reference which is lost to us is hidden in the early Middle English:

> Summe sende ylues
> and summe sende nadderes;
> summe sende nikeres
> the bi den watere wunien.
> Nister man nenne
> bute Ildebrand onne,

an obscure text about water-sprites which is headed *Ita quod dicere possunt cum Wade*. See Bruce Dickins, *Runic and Heroic Poems*, Cambridge, 1915, p. 49.

Das Lied vom Alten Hildebrand

DICHTERISCHE Darstellung, in heroischem Geiste, einer heroischen Begebenheit, die weit in der Vergangenheit liegt; dramatisch zugespitzter heldischer Konflikt in dem die kämpferische Gesinnung mehr wiegt als das eigentliche Kämpfen; geballte Handlung, in der alles Unwesentliche, häufig sogar Exposition, die für unsere Begriffe nicht immer gänzlich entbehrlich ist, ausscheidet; eine dichterische Darstellung, in der wir von Gipfel zu Gipfel schreiten; eine atemlose Folge von Höhepunkten; nichts Beschauliches; nichts Geruhsames; eine unruhige, aufgeregte und aufregende, grell malende Kunst: so ist das germanische Heldenlied.

Diese germanische Heldendichtung lebt in der Fürstenhalle; sie ist Kriegerunterhaltung, nach dem Mahle vor dem Gefolgsherrn und vor der *druht* vorgetragen, von einem Dichter, der selbst Mitglied dieser *druht* ist und der die Ideale der *druht* in seiner Dichtung zu verkörpern trachtet. Diese Dichtung ist demnach Standesdichtung der Kriegerkaste. Sie ist an Zeiten gebunden, in denen ein beherzter Haudegen, von ihm blind ergebenen Kriegern umringt, auszieht, um sich ein Land zu erobern oder um Beute zu erringen und sich dann auf seinen Stammsitz zurückzuziehen. In den südgermanischen Angriffen auf das Römerreich begegnet uns solches Kleinkönigtum selten. Um mit den Römern fertig zu werden, dazu

brauchte es schon grössere Kriegerverbände. In Nord-
germanien jedoch können wir dieses Kleinkönigtum bis
spät in das Mittelalter verfolgen, so bei den Jarlen, die
sich in [19/20] den Orkney- und Shetlandinseln festsetzten.
Allerdings pflegten diese Jarle nicht mehr oder nur ganz
selten noch das altgermanische Heldenlied. Bei ihnen
erklang der skaldische Fürstenpreis. Das Heldenlied war
wohl schon während des 10. Jahrhunderts in den meisten
nordgermanischen Fürstenhöfen als unmodern und
altväterlich verbannt, obgleich sowohl Lebensbedingun-
gen wie kriegerische Ideale in Nordgermanien zu dieser
Zeit wenig verschieden gewesen sein können von denen
der Südgermanen, als sie zur Völkerwanderungszeit gegen
den mittelländischen Kulturraum anstürmten.

Das südgermanische Heldenlied ist Völkerwanderungs-
dichtung und fest mit dieser geschichtlichen Epoche
verbunden. Der Angle Offa regierte um 350, um 375
stirbt der grosse Ostgotenkönig Ermanarich: Offa und
Ermanarich sind die ältesten Namen, die wir als ge-
schichtlich erwiesen in die germanische Heldensage
einreihen können. Der letzte Südgermane, der in die
Heldendichtung eingeht, ist der Langobarde Alboin. Er
wurde 572 ermordet. Der Angle Offa und der Langobarde
Alboin. Sollte das gänzlich Zufall sein? Angeln und
Langobarden waren ursprünglich benachbarte Stämme.
Bei beiden finden wir eine reiche dichterische Ueber-
lieferung.

Wie die germanische Dichtung vor der Völker-
wanderung aussah, wissen wir nicht. Dass es Dichtung
gab, wenn auch nicht notwendigerweise Heldendichtung,
ist sicher. Auch von der Form dieser Dichtung können
wir etwas erschliessen. Nach dem bekannten Tacitäischen
Zeugnis benutzten die Germanen schon zu seiner Zeit den
Stabreim. Nun gibt uns aber Tacitus ein ins Einzelne

gehendes und anschauliches Bild vom Leben und Treiben am Hofe der germanischen Fürsten, die die kriegstüchtige Jugend — die *iuguth*, wie der technische Ausdruck in der altenglischen Epik lautet — um sich versammeln. Wir können der Tacitäischen Darstellung unbedingt trauen. Es war höchst wichtig für Rom, sehr genau zu wissen, was an einem solchen unruhigen, gefährlichen Hofe vor sich ging. Das Verhältnis von Fürst und jungen Kriegern, das uns der Römer nach sicher zuverlässigen Quellen schildert, unterscheidet sich kaum von dem Verhältnis, das wir später in der Völkerwanderungszeit vortreffen. Nur eins fehlt bei [20/21] Tacitus: der Dichter. Das macht uns stutzig. Der Hofdichter, in dessen Liedern das Ethos dieser Kriegergesellschaft hell aufleuchtet, hätte es den gegeben, der Römer hätte nicht geschwiegen. Wir gehen deshalb wohl kaum fehl, wenn wir der Zeit vor der Völkerwanderung den heldischen Hofdichter, den *scop*, absprechen.

Die zwei geschichtlich ältesten germanischen Heldensagenstoffe, die Geschichte von der jugendlichen Heldentat des Angeln Offa und die Geschichte von dem Ende Ermanarichs sehen nicht wie Heldenlieder aus, wenn wir alles hinwegdenken, was aus späterer Ueberlieferung stammt. Der Bericht bei Jordanes von den Brüdern Sarus und Ammius, die den Tod ihrer Schwester an dem greisen König zu rächen versuchen, stammt sicher aus einem Liede, er ist nicht mehr reiner Geschichtsbericht; ob er aber auf ein Heldenlied zurückgeht, bleibt recht zweifelhaft. So, wie der Bericht vorliegt, kommen wir mit dem Begriff 'historisches Lied' gut aus. Sippenfehde und Sippenrache, obwohl sie das eigentlich treibende Moment sind in vielen Heldenliedern, genügen noch nicht, um in der Liedquelle des Jordanes ein Heldenlied zu vermuten. Genau so liegt es bei Offa. Der achtzeilige Bericht im *Widsith* ist faktisch, historisch. Die Freude des Dichters an der jugendlichen Heldentat ist unverkennbar, aber zu einem Heldenliede reicht es nicht aus. Das erhaltene eddische Lied von Hamðir und Sørli, das aus manchen Quellen erschliessbare Offalied zeigen, was der heldische Hofdichter aus diesen Stoffen zu machen wusste, wie er sie enthistorisierte, wie er sie verpersönlichte.

Wir vermuten, dass die eigentliche Heldenlieddichtung während des 5. Jahrhunderts an einem der germanischen Königshöfe einsetzte, dass ein grosser Dichter die neue Gattung auf einen Hieb schuf, und dass sie sich dann rasch ausbreitete. Es ist müssig zu fragen, wo. Unsere Kenntnis reicht bei weitem nicht aus, um diese Frage zu beantworten. Gewöhnlich hat man auf die Goten geraten, und gewiss, viele gotische Stoffe und Helden finden sich in der Ueberlieferung. An frühen Stoffen allerdings haben wir nur das Ende Ermanarichs. Die eigentliche Gotensage ist mit dem Namen und dem Schicksal Dietrichs von Bern verknüpft, und die kann erst nach der Mitte des sechsten Jahrhun- [21/22] derts entstanden sein, als das Gotenreich in Italien schon zerfallen war. Dass das Heldenlied früh gepflegt wurde bei Angeln, Goten, Burgundern und Franken, wissen wir. Für die Angeln zeugt die reiche englische Ueberlieferung, die anglisch ist, nicht sächsisch. Für die Angeln, die südlichen Nachbarn der Nordgermanen, zeugt ferner, dass Stoffe, die im 6. Jahrhundert dichterisch geformt wurden, nicht mehr in Liedform in den Norden drangen. Denn hier müssen die Angeln weitgehend die Vermittler sein. Ihr altes, festländisches Gebiet lag noch zu Anfang des 8. Jahrhunderts brach, wie der Angle Beda in seiner Kirchengeschichte zuverlässig bezeugt.

Burgundische Ueberlieferungen, die später von den Franken übernommen wurden — genau so wie die

Langobarden das dichterische Erbe der Goten antraten —;
waren von Anfang an mit dem Gegenspieler Attila und
seinen Hunnen verknüpft. Attila und die Hunnen sind
nicht aus der ursprünglich südgermanischen Heldensage
wegzudenken, und das mag sehr wohl bedeuten, dass
der geschichtlichen und politischen Verknüpfung von
Hunnen und Germanen auch eine literarische zur Seite
stand. Denn manches in der altgermanischen Dichtung ist
ausgesprochen hunnenfreundlich. Aus den zuverlässigen
Angaben bei Priscos wissen wir, dass es eine hochent-
wickelte hunnische Dichtung gab. Chorische Preislieder
der Mädchen, von langsamem Tanz begleitet, Preislieder
oder gar historische Lieder, von zwei Barbaren bei einem
besonders festlichen Gastmahl vor Attila vorgetragen,
ein preisendes Totenlied auf den grossen Hunnenkönig,
dessen Inhalt uns Jordanes, der hier Priscos ausschreibt,
übermittelt: im Grunde wissen wir mehr von der frühen
hunnischen Dichtung als von der frühen germanischen.
Man überschätze nicht die Feindschaft zwischen Hunnen
und Germanen zur Völkerwanderungszeit. Der gemein-
same Feind war Rom. Ost-West-Gegensätze waren
weniger wichtig. Der freundliche Attila, der schliesslich
in die milde Gestalt im *Nibelungenlied* ausmündete,
überlebte den Zusammenbruch des Hunnenreiches. Goten
und Gepiden räumten mit den Attilasöhnen auf, doch der
Vater blieb der grosse Herrscher und der grosse Freund.
Man kann nicht ohne weiteres behaupten, der freundliche
Attila sei von den [22/23] Goten übermittelt worden. Der
freundliche Attila ist weitgehend südgermanisch, sein
Reich erstreckt sich fast bis an den Rhein, und nur von
den 437 noch rechtsrheinischen Burgundern können wir
annehmen, sie hätten nach dem Zusammenbruch in Attila
den finsteren Feind gesehen. Dieses burgundische
Attilabild eignete auch den linksrheinischen Franken und

5

durch das Heldenlied kam der grausame Hunnenfürst zu
den Nordgermanen.

Zur Zeit Attilas sassen die Langobarden in Niederöster-
reich. Sie waren bestimmt Attila tributpflichtig, und wir
haben nicht den geringsten Grund anzunehmen, ihr
Attilabild sei ein unfreundliches gewesen. Die Gemahlin
Alboins war eine gepidische Prinzessin, viele Gepiden
hatten sich den Langobarden angeschlossen bei ihrem
Zuge nach Italien. Dort stiessen Goten zu ihnen. Lango-
barden, Gepiden, Goten: sie alle hatten ein freundliches
Attilabild.

Die eigentliche Heldenlieddichtung setzt während des
5. Jahrhunderts an einem der südgermanischen Fürsten-
höfe ein. Das kann nur heissen: das germanische
Heldenlied wurde um diese Zeit von einem grossen
Dichter in einem Ruck geschaffen. Dieser Dichter, sicher
am mehr historisch gehaltenen Lied geschult, wandte
allem rein Politischen und Historischen resolut den
Rücken. Er versetzte seine Fabel in eine zeitentrückte
Vergangenheit, schuf sie im allgemeinen aus geschicht-
lichem Stoff, manchmal, wie im *Hildebrandslied*, griff er
eine Wanderfabel auf und versah sie mit einem geschicht-
lich bekannten Hintergrund; er liess das Politische fallen,
und die Geschichte wurde bei ihm zur Sippenfehde und
zum Sippenverrat. Dieses einfache Schema beschränkte
die Zahl der auftretenden Personen, und man kann
wirklich von dem Auftreten der Personen reden, wie in
einem Drama, denn das eigentlich vorwärtstreibende
Element in der Handlung sind grösstenteils die Reden,
und auch das, was wir von der Vorgeschichte wissen
müssen, wird zum grossen Teile durch die Reden der
handelnden Personen vermittelt wie im griechischen
Chor. Das typische und am grossartigsten durchdachte
Beispiel dieser Art ist das *Hildebrandslied*.

Es lag dem Dichter nichts daran, aus dem germanischen Gesichtskreis herauszutreten. Der grosse geschichtliche Feind [23/24] war Rom: von Rom hören wir im Heldenlied nichts, nur der sprichwörtliche Reichtum des römischen Kaisers wird gelegentlich erwähnt, und das ist dann der oströmische Kaiser. Die Hunnen gehören für den Heldenlieddichter mit zur germanischen Gemeinschaft. Man hat in dem wilden Atli der *Atlakviða* germanischen Abscheu vor asiatischer Unmenschlichkeit entdecken wollen und Aehnliches behauptet man vielfach von dem Hunnenbild in der *Hunnenschlacht*. Ist Nidud der Niarenfürst etwa weniger wild oder ist die Rache, die Wieland an ihm nimmt, etwa menschlicher?

Der Heldenlieddichter befasst sich also nur mit dem innergermanischen Raum. Dies kann doch wohl nur heissen, dass Fürst und Gefolge, seine Zuhörerschaft, es so wollen. Für sie ist der Römer kein seelisches Problem. Streit im Stamm und Fehde in der Sippe: es ist das Naheliegende, das Lokale, von dem die Zuhörerschaft zu hören wünscht. Der germanische Krieger hat keinen weiten Horizont. Er aber bestimmt die Themen. Gewiss, der Dichter ist dem einfachen Krieger überlegen an künstlerischer Gestaltungskraft und im Nacherleben seelischer Konflikte; doch dichtet er für den Zuhörerkreis, er ist fest an ihn gebunden, und der Geschmack des Publikums, wie wir sagen würden, bestimmt letzten Endes, was der Dichter seinen Zuhörern bieten kann.

Der Dichter schafft das Heldenlied, es findet Anklang, es wird Mode, es verbreitet sich rasch von Stamm zu Stamm. Dieses Wandern kann man sich ursprünglich nur vorstellen als das Wandern des *scop* von einem Hofe zum anderen. Ein sehr idealisiertes Bild eines solchen Herumwanderns liefert uns der *Widsith*, in dem ein *scop* aus dem Stamme der Myrginge vom festländischen anglischen

Hofe an den Gotenhof zieht. Wer diese Myrginge waren ist nicht sicher auszumachen, jedenfalls lebten sie im anglischen Raume in Norddeutschland und gingen zu Offas Zeiten oder ein wenig später im anglischen Königreiche auf.

Diese Heldendichtung war gesprochene, deklamierte Dichtung. Sie lebte einzig und allein im Vortrag. Niedergeschrieben wurde sie sicher nicht. Weder konnte der Dichter schreiben noch konnten die Zuhörer lesen. Das weiss man; doch lohnt es, sich dies immer wieder ins Gedächtnis zurückzurufen. Das Nieder- [24/25] schreiben erfolgt später, wohl immer aus antiquarischem Interesse. Es ist nicht etwa Ungunst des Schicksals, dass uns so wenig erhalten ist. Es ist im Gegenteil eine ganz besondere Gunst, dass wir überhaupt Niederschriften besitzen. Abgesehen von diesen wenigen Niederschriften sind wir auf Anspielungen, Nacherzählungen bei Chronisten und ganz späte Epen angewiesen. Schreiben konnte nur der Geistliche. Er stand der Heldendichtung gewiss nicht immer feindlich gegenüber, doch kam es ihm meistens garnicht in den Sinn, derartige Dichtung in Buchform zu sammeln.

In Island lagen die Verhältnisse wesentlich anders. Nicht nur gab es dort im 13. Jahrhundert noch eine einigermassen lebendige Heldenliedüberlieferung, sondern man gab sich auch die Mühe, diese Heldenlieder aufzuschreiben. Die englischen Sammelhandschriften hingegen pflegen im allgemeinen die geistliche, christliche Dichtung. Im *Vercelli-codex* und *Junius-codex* finden wir nichts Germanisches, der *Beowulf* im *Cottonischen Codex* ist zwar ein unschätzbares Zeugnis für die Vorzeit, aus dem wir manch sicheren Rückschluss machen können: germanisches Heldenlied ist er aber nicht. Der *Exeter-codex* bringt *Widsith* und *Sängers Trost*. Beide Gedichte sind kostbare Fundgruben aber auch sie sind keine Heldenlieder. Einzig und allein das *Finnsburg-fragment* führt uns unmittelbar in eine ältere und wildere Zeit zurück. Die Sammlung, die, wie glaubwürdig berichtet wird, Karl der Grosse anlegen liess, ist nicht erhalten. Man braucht nicht anzunehmen, sie sei bewusst vernichtet worden. Die Schriftkundigen hatten keinen Grund, eine solche Sammlung besonders zu hüten und so ging sie uns, wie so manches andere, verloren. Ob diese wohl grösstenteils fränkische Sammlung auch das *Hildebrandslied* brachte, ist sehr fraglich.

Als einziges direktes deutsches Zeugnis liegt uns das Fragment des *Hildebrandsliedes* vor. Es ist das bei weitem älteste erhaltene germanische heroische Lied. Die Niederschrift des *Finnsburgliedes*, von der wir leider nur eine Kopie haben, stammt sprachlichen Anzeichen nach aus dem elften Jahrhundert, ist also über 300 Jahre später als das *Hildebrandslied* niedergeschrieben. Was uns auf Island gerettet ist, wurde wohl gut 450 bis 500 [25/26] Jahre nach dem *Hildebrandslied* aufgezeichnet. Von dem Inhalt ganz abgesehen, verleiht schon dieses ehrwürdige Alter dem Fragment eine zentrale Stellung in der Heldenliedforschung. Soweit wir dies ermessen können, kann das Original der Dichtung schwerlich viel mehr als 200 Jahre vor der Niederschrift zuerst vorgetragen worden sein. Beim *Finnsburgliede* müssen wir schon mit weit über 300 Jahren rechnen, und bei den eddischen Heldenliedern, die aus Südgermanien eingewandert sind, muss man für die südgermanischen Vorlagen mit einem Zeitraum von mindestens 700 Jahren rechnen. Hinzu kommt, dass diese norwegischisländischen Heldenlieder schon aus rein sprachlichen Gründen stärkere Aenderungen haben erfahren müssen als die zwei im Süden erhaltenen Fragmente.

So ist das Material, aus dem wir das klassische Helden-
lied der späten Völkerwanderungszeit zu erschliessen
haben. Kein Wunder, dass unter den Heldenliedforschern
der Streit der Meinungen andauert.

Das *Hildebrandslied* wurde wie bekannt etwa um 810-820
in dem von den angelsächsischen Missionsmönchen
gegründeten Kloster Fulda niedergeschrieben. Kaum von
Angelsachsen. Dagegen spricht schon die reichlich
primitive Form der w-Rune. Diese w-Rune erscheint aber
sehr häufig, und man könnte meinen, die Vorlage sei von
einem Angelsachsen geschrieben worden, besonders da
auch ein insulares *F* erscheint. Sicherheit ist hier nicht zu
gewinnen. Kluge hat einmal unternommen zu beweisen,
das *Hildebrandslied* sei in einem einheitlichen Dialekt
geschrieben. Der Versuch musste scheitern.

So, wie das Gedicht vor uns liegt, kann es nie
vorgetragen worden sein. Die Sprache ist grausam
verhunzt. Oberdeutsch, Fränkisch, das Ganze mit
niederdeutschen Formen vermengt und übertüncht, so
liegt das einzige erhaltene deutsche Heldenlied vor uns.
Ueber die unglaubliche Mischung sind sich heutzutage
wohl alle Forscher einig, aber wie diese Mischung
entstanden sein mag, über diese Frage wird man schwer-
lich jemals ins Reine kommen. Früher glaubte mancher
Gelehrter, das Lied sei von Norden nach Süden gewan-
dert; sogar an angel-sächsischen Ursprung dachte man.
Heute wissen wir, dass es vom Süden nach [26/27] dem
Norden wandert, und dass es eine bairische Zwischenstufe
gegeben haben muss. Eine rein philologische Analyse
führt uns nicht über einen bairischen Text zurück, den
wir um 750 datieren. Ob dieses bairische Lied nur
mündlich umlief oder, ob es schon damals schriftlich
fixiert wurde, auch über diese Frage ist unter den
Forschern keine Einigkeit zu erzielen. Jedenfalls muss

man dem Befund unserer Handschrift nach mit einer
bairischen Niederschrift rechnen, und diese Niederschrift
ist für uns der Anfang — und das Ende! — der schrift-
lichen Ueberlieferung. Man glaubt allgemein, die Schrei-
ber hätten die Niederschrift abgebrochen, weil kein Platz
mehr vorhanden gewesen sei. Das stimmt wohl nicht. Es
war noch Platz für einige Zeilen, schliesslich hätte man
auch am Rande schreiben können. Will man nicht
annehmen, die Arbeit sei irgendwie unterbrochen und
dann nie wieder aufgenommen worden, so ist wohl
wahrscheinlicher, die Vorlage selbst sei fragmentarisch
gewesen.

Wie dem auch sein mag, eine Vorlage lässt sich mit
grösster Wahrscheinlichkeit erweisen, da die Wörter
«darba gistuontun» zweimal erscheinen. In Vers 23 steht
in der Handschrift: «d& sid detrihhe darba gistuontum»,
in Vers 26b glitt das Auge des Abschreibers auf das
«detrihhe» in Vers 23 zurück und er schrieb: «unti
deotrichhe darba gistontun». «unti» für «miti» ist ein
bekannter, nicht weiter ernst zu nehmender Fehler, die
verschiedene Schreibung von «gistuontun» ist schon
gewichtiger; innerhalb von acht Zeilen finden wir die
folgenden Schreibungen für Dietrich: 19 «theotrihhe»,
23 «detrihhe», 26 «deotrichhe» und vor dem «sid» von
Vers 23 ein den meisten von uns unverständliches
«d&», das doch wohl eine Vorwegnahme von «detrihhe»
ist. Schreibung von Eigennamen besagt nicht viel, es ist
aber bemerkenswert, dass der Schreiber Dietrich jedesmal
anders buchstabiert. Es sieht nicht so aus, als ob man sich
ohne weiteres auf die zwei Schreiber verlassen könne.
Und doch ist auf die Schreiber mehr Verlass als auf
moderne Gelehrte, die sich nicht genug tun können und
die immer lustig weiter verbessern. Das Braunesche
Lesebuch verzeichnet bei weitem nicht alle vorgeschla-

genen Konjekturen, doch selbst das, was es bietet, ist eine verwirrende Fülle von scharfsin- [27/28] nigen und unsinnigen Verbesserungen und Schlimmbesserungen, mit denen die Herausgeber einmal gründlich aufräumen sollten. Fast 150 Jahre lang hat man fleissig emendiert, und was ist dabei herausgekommen? Abgesehen von rein orthographischen Aenderungen, nehmen die Herausgeber selten mehr als ein halbes Dutzend dieser Verbesserungen in ihre Textausgaben auf.

So wie uns das Lied in der Handschrift entgegentritt, bietet es uns manchen sinnlosen Fehler, wahrscheinlich einige Lücken, umgestellte Zeilen, ernsthafte Verstösse gegen die Gesetze der Alliteration, Stellen die wie Prosa aussehen, viele kleinere Ungenauigkeiten, und all dies in einem vollkommen unmöglichen sprachlichen Kauderwelsch. Trotz alledem: hinter diesem Fragment erfühlt man die straffe, mit vollendeter Meisterschaft aufgebaute dramatische Handlung, hier ersteht vor uns ein erschütternder innerer Kampf in der Seele des verzweifelten Vaters, der gezwungen ist, dem ungläubigen Sohne mit der Waffe in der Hand entgegenzutreten, hier haben wir ein in seiner Art unübertroffenes literarisches Kunstwerk des späten Völkerwanderungszeitalters und, vom Standpunkt der Zuhörer gesehen, hier haben wir eine Kriegergesellschaft, die Verständnis hat für die Seelennot des Kriegers, der zwischen zwei Pflichten steht.

Der Schluss fehlt. Dass der Vater den Sohn tötet, lässt sich aus der ganzen Anlage erschliessen. Zum Ueberfluss haben wir andere Quellen, die uns diesen Ausgang bestätigen. Wie die Tötung des Sohnes von dem germanischen Dichter motiviert wurde, wissen wir allerdings nicht. Der unbekannte Dichter schaltete völlig frei mit dem Vater-Sohnkampf-Motiv, und wir sind nicht gerechtfertigt, aus den irischen, persischen und russischen

Parallelen Rückschlüsse auf das *Hildebrandslied* zu ziehen. Das spätere deutsche in der *Þiðrekssaga* erhaltene Lied und das *Jüngere Hildebrandslied* helfen nicht weiter. Man hat viel Aufhebens gemacht von dem sogenannten feigen Schlag, der in diesen jungen deutschen Quellen erscheint. Er lässt sich aus der *Þiðrekssaga* herauslesen und aus dem Ausruf des bärbeissigen Alten im *Jüngeren Hildebrandslied*: «den slac lert dich ein wip». Aber sowohl die *Þiðrekssaga* sowie das *Jüngere Hildebrandslied* stehen mittelbar unter dem Einfluss der höfischen Literatur des [28/29] Hochmittelalters, und wir dürfen nur mit grossem Vorbehalt folgern, Hadubrand sei ursprünglich eines feigen Schlages wegen von seinem Vater getötet worden. Gewiss, Hadubrand schiebt Hildebrand betrügerische Absichten unter, wenn er sagt: «pist also gialtet man so du ewin inwit fortos», d.h. «du hast es nur deiner Verschlagenheit zu verdanken, dass du überhaupt noch am Leben bist». Dass er sich dann selbst später im Kampfe einer Kriegslist bedient, dieses wirksame Motiv trauen wir dem Dichter durchaus zu. Ehrenrührig war solche List nicht. Die Germanen der Völkerwanderungszeit werden sich in dieser Hinsicht wenig von den Isländern unterschieden haben, die für heldenhaftes Verhalten Sinn hatten, die es aber auch nicht verschmähten, einem Feind das Haus über dem Kopf anzustecken und ihn aus sicherem Hinterhalt niederzustrecken, wenn er trachtete, aus dem brennenden Gebäude zu entkommen.

Die Kriegslist hat aber ihren regelrechten Platz im Vater-Sohnkampf. In der irischen Sage tötet Cuchullin seinen Sohn Conla mit einer furchtbaren und für unsere Begriffe niederträchtigen Waffe, nachdem er dreimal dem Sohn unterlegen ist: beim Schwertkampf, beim Ringen und beim Schwimmen. Der Sohn ruft aus: «Meine Mutter hat mich nicht über diese Waffe belehrt». Dies ist allerdings eine bemerkenswerte Parallele zum *Jüngeren Hilde-brandslied*. Wie wir uns diese Parallele zu erklären haben, ist eine schwierige Frage und es wäre fruchtlos, sich an dieser Stelle eingehend mit diesem Rätsel zu beschäftigen. Die Parallele kann sich durch reinen Zufall ergeben haben. Auch darf man den Unterschied nicht unbetont lassen, dass es im irischen Lied der Sohn ist, der auf die Waffe des Vaters anspielt.

In der persischen Erzählung rettet sich der völlig geschlagene Vater durch eine List. Am nächsten Tage erschlägt er den Sohn. Nur in der russischen Ballade hören wir etwas von Hinterlist des Sohnes, der dort versucht, den schlafenden Vater mit einer Lanze zu durchbohren. Die Lanze gleitet vom Kreuz ab, das der Vater auf der Brust trägt. Er erwacht und tötet seinen Sohn. Diese russische Ballade ist bestimmt die späteste von allen Versionen. Manche abwegige Motive finden sich in ihr verarbeitet, und auf sie allein gestützt, kann man nicht wagen, sich den Schluss des [29/30] germani-schen Liedes zurechtzulegen. «Lieber ein toter Sohn als ein lebender Feigling» ist ein modernes Phantasiebild, das besser in die unwirkliche Welt des ritterlichen Hochmit-telalters passt als in das alte Germanien. Dass einer der beiden Helden sterben muss, wissen wir; dass es der Sohn ist, der fällt, wissen wir auch. Wie dieser Tod aber motiviert war, entzieht sich unserer Kenntnis.

Das *Hildebrandslied* ist nicht typisch für die Gattung des Heldenliedes. Es wächst über sie hinaus. In allen anderen Heldenliedern haben wir eine Handlung, in die die Hauptpersonen tief verwickelt sind. Vergeltung eines angetanen Unrechts oder einer erlittenen Schmach, Blutrache, Goldgier, Erbstreitigkeiten: das sind die Motive. Fast immer sind es Verwandte, die einander gegenüberstehen, häufig durch Heirat verwandte Helden.

So rückt die Frau, die auf beiden Seiten Verwandte hat, in den Mittelpunkt. Beispiele finden sich im *Finnsburglied*, im *Ingeldlied*, im Lied vom Tode Siegfrieds, im Burgundenuntergang. Trotzdem kann man kaum behaupten, der Frau falle im Heldenlied eine zentrale Rolle zu. Allerdings scheint es, als ob der Frau im Burgundenuntergang von jeher grössere Bedeutung zukam. Ob diese Rolle jedoch ursprünglich so bedeutend war wie man nach dem *Atlamál* vermuten könnte, ist eine andere Sache. Da fast immer Blutsverwandte und Verschwägerte einander gegenüberstehen, ist Verletzung der Blutbande fast eine Selbstverständlichkeit. Hierin fügt sich das *Hildebrandslied* dem allgemeinen Schema ein, obwohl, und das ist höchst wichtig, Vater und Sohn nicht den geringsten persönlichen Grund zum Streit haben. Wo kein persönlicher Anreiz zum Kampfe vorliegt — dieser persönliche Grund zum Kampfe schliesst selbstverständlich das Treueband zum Fürsten ein — da kann im allgemeinen kein Zusammenprall erfolgen von der Art, die den Heldenlieddichter anzieht.

Im *Hildebrandslied* treffen sich die Helden entweder ganz zufällig — und das ist die Situation die in der *Þiðrekssaga* und im *Jüngeren Hildebrandslied* vorliegt — oder aber die Helden sind ausgewählt worden, um durch ihren Kampf entweder die Schlacht zu entscheiden oder um den allgemeinen Kampf einzuleiten. Dass es sich nicht etwa um eine zufällige Begegnung handelt, ist völlig [30/31] klar von der ganzen Anlage der Einleitung. Beide Helden sind Erheisser, Herausheisser, Herausforderer, Kempen. Sie prüfen sorgfältig ihre Ausrüstung, waffnen sich, gürten die Schwerter dann über die Panzerhemden und reiten zum Kampfplatz. Es handelt sich also hier um einen vertraglich festgelegten Kampf von zwei ausgesuchten Helden. Beide Heere schauen zu. Wir dürfen

annehmen, die Kempen sind die Anführer der beiden
Heere; zum mindesten müssen wir annehmen, sie seien
die Haupthelden von Theoderich und Odoaker. Von den
Heeren selbst hören wir nichts mehr. Doch dürfen wir
nicht ausser Acht lassen, dass sie da sind, als schweigsame
und aufmerksame Zuschauer, die jedes Wort, das
gesprochen wird, hören und wägen. Dies lässt sich alles
aus dem Gedicht selbst ersehen, denn dieses Gedicht,
abgesehen von der Dietrich-Einlage, verlangt weit
weniger Wissen um die Zusammenhänge, von den zwei
Heeren und von uns, als allgemein in der Heldendichtung
üblich ist. Das Gedicht ist nicht voll von dunklen und
weithergeholten Anspielungen. Alles wird erklärt, ab-
gesehen von dem Grunde, warum die zwei Heere
überhaupt einander gegenüberstehen. Und auch das lässt
sich allmählich aus dem Gedicht selbst erschliessen und
wäre vermutlich völlig klar, hätten wir das Ende.

Das Gedicht ist daher vollkommen auf sich gestellt. Es
ist nicht eine Episode in dem Heldenleben Hildebrands
oder auch Hadubrands. Alles, was wir über diese zwei
Helden wissen oder zu wissen brauchen, finden wir in
dem uns vorliegenden Gedicht. Was das spätere Mittel-
alter von Hildebrand zu wissen vorgibt, darüber brauchen
wir uns keine Gedanken zu machen.

Das Motiv vom Zweikampf, der den Völkerstreit
entscheiden soll, ist ein altes, es ist aber wohl kaum ein
germanisches. Es erübrigt sich, hier eingehend über die
vielen Parallelen zu handeln. Greifen wir nur das allge-
mein Bekannte und Naheliegende heraus.

Im Alten Testament haben wir den Zweikampf von
David und Goliath. David bedient sich einer etwas
ungewöhnlichen Waffe, von der Goliath nichts weiss, und
gegen die er sich infolgedessen nicht verteidigen kann.
Aus Livius kennen wir die Geschichte von den drei

römischen Brüdern, die gegen drei [31/32] Brüder aus dem feindlichen Lager kämpfen. Der Sieg soll den Krieg entscheiden. Zwei Römer fallen, der dritte flieht. Die jubelnden Feinde verfolgen ihn. Wenn die drei Verfolger bei der Flucht auseinandergeraten sind, wendet sich der Römer und tötet alle drei. Diesmal keine ungewöhnliche Waffe sondern eine Kriegslist. Wir haben schon erwähnt, dass im persischen, irischen und russischen Vater-Sohnkampf der List auch eine entscheidende Rolle zufällt. In den verabredeten, meistens sich vor Augenzeugen abspielenden Zweikämpfen spielt also häufig eine ungewöhnliche Waffe oder eine Kriegslist eine ausschlaggebende Rolle.

In der germanischen Dichtung ist der politisch bedingte Zweikampf nicht gerade häufig. Abgesehen vom *Hildebrandslied* haben wir ihn vielleicht in der ursprünglichen Fassung des *Offaliedes*, doch sieht man dort nicht klar; die *Widsith*-Stelle bleibt zu mehrdeutig. Auch in der germanischen Geschichte begegnet uns ein derartiger Zweikampf nicht allzuoft. In der *Germania* Kapitel 10 berichtet Tacitus von dem Brauch, einen Gefangenen aus dem feindlichen Heere vollbewaffnet einem der Eigenen gegenüberzustellen. So wollte man den Ausgang des bevorstehenden Kampfes erfahren. Also Orakel, nicht politische Massnahme. Bei Fredegar lesen wir zum Jahre 604 die schöne Geschichte von dem tapferen Franken Bertoald, der gewillt ist, gegen Landerich zu kämpfen. Es scheint so, als ob dieser Kampf den allgemeinen Streitfall entscheiden solle. Beide Kämpfer sollten, von ihren Heeren getrennt, miteinander kämpfen. Der *major domus* Landerich aber drückte sich, Bertoald und ein kleines Gefolge waren durch diese List von ihrer Hauptmacht getrennt, und wurden von den Gegnern niedergemetzelt.

Bei Gregor von Tours wird erzählt von dem Kampfe zweier *pueri* im Kriege zwischen Vandalen und Alemannen. Der vandalische *puer* wird besiegt und die Alemannen räumen das Feld. Hier hören wir nichts von List. Wohl aber erscheint die List wiederum bei Fredegar zum Jahre 629. Der Kaiser Heraklios soll statt des ganzen Heeres gegen den persischen Kaiser Kosdroes kämpfen. Der Perser schickt einen Vertreter, und dieser fällt durch eine Kriegslist. [32/33].

Und nun noch einige Beispiele bei dem Langobarden Paulus Diaconus. Die Langobarden wollen durch das Gebiet der Assipites ziehen. Das Recht des Durchzugs soll durch einen Einzelkampf erkauft werden. Ein Sklave ist bereit zu kämpfen, wenn man ihm die Freiheit verspricht. Er siegt und die Langobarden erhalten freien Durchzug. Von dem Könige Lamissio erzählt Paulus eine ähnliche Geschichte. Der König trifft mitten im Fluss eine Amazone, die er tötet. Die Langobarden dürfen hierauf unbehindert den Fluss überschreiten. Im Kriege mit Alachis will Kuninkbert den Streitfall im Einzelkampf mit Alachis beilegen. Alachis weigert sich, und Kuninkbert wiederholt sein Angebot. Alachis weigert sich noch immer, und die Schlacht beginnt, in der Alachis unterliegt. Bei Paulus Diaconus, dem Langobarden, finden sich also drei Fälle von politisch motiviertem Zweikampf.

Die germanischen Parallelen spielen sich sämtlich auf altem, klassischem Boden ab. In Griechenland und Rom, in der *polis* und der *res publica*, wo der Einzelne der Stadt oder dem Staat tief verpflichtet war, konnten sich solche Anschauungen leicht entwickeln. Die römische Geschichte bietet uns immer wieder Beispiele von Römern, die sich für den Staat opfern. Der Germane kannte von Haus aus kein so fest gefügtes Staatengebilde. Ihm galt

Treue zum Stammeshäuptling mehr als alles rein Politische. Gewiss war er bereit, für seinen Häuptling zu sterben, aber für ihn einen Zweikampf auszufechten, wäre ihm als absurd erschienen. Das hätte der Häuptling auch nie zulassen können. Wir dürfen deshalb mit grosser Wahrscheinlichkeit vermuten, dass Geschichten von derartigen politischen Zweikämpfen den Germanen erst auf Römerboden bekannt wurden. Wir merken uns auch, dass es bei solchen Zweikämpfen keinen Pardon geben kann. Einer der beiden Kempen muss fallen.

Diesen politischen Zweikampf, der hier auch noch zu einem Vater-Sohnkampf gesteigert ist, baut der Dichter ein in die Geschichte von Dietrichs Flucht. Hier müssen wir annehmen, dass die Zuhörer wissen, wer Dietrich ist, wer Odoaker, wer Attila, und was es mit dieser Geschichte für eine Bewandtnis hat. Wir wissen es leider nicht. Wie berühmt Dietrich auch [33/34] geworden sein mag, und wie viel wir auch sowohl von ihm wie von seinem geschichtlichen Vorbild wissen, und trotz des grossen Scharfsinnes so vieler Heldensagenforscher sind wir nicht in der Lage, eine zufriedenstellende, heldische Geschichte zu konstruieren. Dietrichs Flucht und Dietrichs Rückkehr bleiben für uns schattenhaft und unwirklich. Dietrichs siegreicher Einzug in sein Stammland nach einem unfreiwilligen Exil von 30 Jahren hätte eine kriegerische Angelegenheit sein müssen mit Schlachtengetümmel und verständlicher Handlung. Man denkt an die Art, wie die Schwedenkriege im *Beowulf* vorgeführt werden mit einem Hintergrund von Massenkampf und der vor dem Massenkampf sich abspielenden Einzelleistung. Dass Heldenlieder so etwas panoramisch darstellen konnten, lernen wir aus der *Hunnenschlacht* und dem *Finnsburglied*. Wir finden nichts dergleichen in der Ueberlieferung.

Genau so liegt es mit der Flucht. Die Motivierung der
Flucht bleibt uns unverständlich. Das allererste, das wir
über diesen grossen Helden in der Sage erfahren, ist, dass
er seinem Widersacher Odoaker entflieht. Helden fliehen
nicht, wenigstens nicht in der Heldensage. Hunderte von
Jahren später sind uns ausgezeichnete Gründe für diese
Flucht überliefert: es war ein selbst auferlegtes Exil, das
Dietrich auf sich nahm, um seine verräterisch von
Ermenrich gefangenen Krieger zu befreien. Im späteren
Mittelalter ist dieses grossmütige Verhalten verständlich,
es passt aber herzlich schlecht in das kriegerische Ethos
der altgermanischen adligen Kriegerkaste. In der Helden-
dichtung befreit man gefangene Freunde mit der Waffe in
der Hand oder man kommt beim Versuch um. Können
wir der germanischen Halle diese hochherzige, rührselige
Geschichte zutrauen? Kaum.

Im *Hildebrandslied* haben wir den ältesten Bericht über
die Exilgeschichte. Aus dem, was uns das Lied erzählt,
können wir jedoch keine vernünftige Handlung zurecht-
stutzen. Von freiwilliger Landräumung ist keine Rede.
Hildebrand entwich dem mörderischen Hass Odoakers
zusammen mit Dietrich und vielen der Dietrichmannen.
Ein ganzer Haufe der floh? So steht es im Text, schwarz
auf weiss, und wir müssen uns damit abfin- [34/35] den,
so gut wie wir können. Und mindestens einer dieses
Haufens liess Frau und Kind elend und allein sitzen, der
Rache des Feindes ausgeliefert. Das aber ist sicher eine
Erfindung unseres Dichters, denn er ist es ja, der über-
haupt erst Hildebrand mit Dietrich in Verbindung brachte.

Und damit kommen wir zum Herz der Untersuchung.
Dieser Dichter band sich nicht eng an die Ueberlieferung.
Er erfand zwar nicht neue Motive, doch baute er aus ihm
bekannten Motiven seine eigene Geschichte auf. Er
kannte den Vater-Sohnkampf und seinen tragischen

Ausgang, an den er unbedingt gebunden war, er kannte auch Geschichten von Einzelkämpfen, die politische Entscheidungen herbeiführten. Aus diesen beiden Erzähltypen baute er seine Fabel. In den anderen Versionen zieht der Sohn aus, um den Vater zu suchen; er hat ein Erkennungszeichen bei sich, das der Mutter bei der ursprünglichen Trennung von Vater und Mutter überantwortet worden war. Die Mutter gibt es dem Sohne auf die Vatersuche mit. Das Erkennungzeichen, das in den anderen Versionen etwas gezwungen ist und immer auf irgend eine Art verborgen bleiben muss, bis es zu spät ist, lässt der Dichter aus. Bei ihm trifft der Vater den Sohn bei der Rückkehr und das ist ganz sicher seine Umdeutung. Er gibt seinen Helden auch Namen, die bis zu diesem Augenblick in der germanischen Dichtung unbekannt waren: Hildebrand und Hadubrand. Sogar ein Grossvater Heribrand wird von ihm erfunden. Dieser Grossvater spielt in der späteren Epik eine etwas schattenhafte Rolle. Doch weiss noch der Wolfdietrich, dass er der Vater Hildebrands war. Von Hadubrand wissen wir nichts, ausser was wir hier und in den jüngeren Versionen erfahren. Er ist nur da, um von seinem Vater erschlagen zu werden. Hildebrand jedoch, der tragische Vater, der an der Leiche des einzigen Sohnes steht, wurde sofort berühmt, und bald war er unlöslich mit Dietrich verbunden. Man baute ihn in die verschiedenen Abenteuer ein, und es ist sehr wohl möglich, dass er so in Abenteuer verstrickt wurde, die schon vor dem *Hildebrandsliede* im Umlauf waren. Damit ist nicht gesagt, dass es vor dem Liede in der Heldendichtung einen Hildebrand gab. Aber wo Dietrich erschien, konnte man Hildebrand später nicht auslassen. [35/36].

Vor einigen Jahren erschien in *Paul und Braunes Beiträgen* 67 ein Aufsatz von Elisabeth Karg-Gasterstädt

6

über die schwierige Stelle im *Hildebrandslied* 23 f.: «sid
Detrihhe darba gistuontun fateres (HS: fatereres) mines».
Man hat immer angenommen, dass dies entweder heisst:
«Dietrich hatte meinen Vater nötig», d.h. «mein Vater
stand ihm hülfreich zur Seite», oder aber: «Es entstanden
Abwesenheiten meines Vaters von Dietrich», d.h.
«Dietrich musste sehen, wie er ohne meinen Vater
zurechtkam». Die zweite Auslegung, von dem grossen
Lachmann bevorzugt, wich allmählich der ersten. Man
hatte die spätere Sagengeschichte im Kopfe, und man
wusste, dass Dietrich und Hildebrand unzertrennliche
Waffengefährten waren. Frau Karg-Gasterstädt, die sich
auf das anderen Germanisten vollkommen unzugängliche
Material für das grosse *Althochdeutsche Wörterbuch* stützen
kann, war in der Lage, rein lexikalisch mit Sicherheit zu
erweisen, dass nur die zweite Deutung möglich sei. Im
Althochdeutschen hat «darba» immer den Sinn von
privatio. Es ist das Gegenteil von «haba»: Besitz, und
daher bedeutet es immer «etwas nicht besitzen», «Beraubt-
sein einer bestimmten Eigenschaft, die dem Subject im
normalen Zustande zukommt». Zwanzig Beispiele aus
Notker erhärten die Deutung. Aehnliche Bedeutungen
werden erschlossen für «tharben», «githarben», «tharbon»,
und das schwache maskulinum «tharbo»: «einer, der an
etwas Mangel leidet, etwas nicht hat, entbehrt». Das
Essener Evangeliar liefert das Adjectivum tharfag:
Mangel, Entbehrung leidend und in dem Ausdruck
tharfag uuerðan als Uebersetzung von *indigere* haben
wir einen sehr ähnlichen Ausdruck wie «darba gistuontun».
Frau Karg-Gasterstädt schliesst: «Welcher Art die
Trennung war, durch die Dietrich seines Waffenmeisters
verlustig ging, mögen die Sagengeschichtler ausfindig
machen. Mir scheint die Auffassung Francks, Hadubrand
spiele auf den Tod seines Vater an, sehr einleuchtend,

doch könnte der Plural «darba» auch auf wiederholte Trennungen deuten, deren Ursache dann doch wohl selbständige Kriegsfahrten Hildebrands — vgl. etwa Hadubrands «her was eo folches at ente» oder sein [36/37] eigenes «dar man mih eo scerita in folc sceotantero» — gewesen sein dürften».

Wir brauchen die Sagengeschichtler nicht weiter zu bemühen. Weder zur Zeit, als das Lied gedichtet wurde noch nachher, gab es «selbständige Kriegsfahrten» Hildebrands. Die von Franck vor über 50 Jahren vorgeschlagene Deutung ist sicher die richtige.

So wie wir den Text haben, ergreift Hadubrand zweimal das Wort. Seine erste Rede erstreckt sich über 15 Zeilen, von 15 bis 29. Die zweite Rede fängt mit Zeile 37 an und endet mit Zeile 44. Es ist jedoch glaubhaft, dass die Zeilen 46–48, die von der Handschrift Hildebrand zugewiesen werden, in Wirklichkeit Hadubrand angehören, und dass sie nach Zeile 40 oder 41 einzusetzen sind. Damit würde die zweite Rede Hadubrands 11 Zeilen lang.

In der Einleitung erfahren wir die Namen der Herausforderer und ihre Verwandtschaft. Auch dass Hildebrand der Vater ist, können die Zuhörer erschliessen, ehe er zu reden beginnt, denn er ist der ältere, lebenserfahrenere. Die erste Rede des Sohnes ist ein Meisterwerk der Exposition. Sie gibt uns alles, was wir von den Beiden zu wissen brauchen, sie zeigt uns einen arglosen Mann in reifem Alter, denn ein Jüngling ist Hadubrand nicht, der ohne irgend welche Hintergedanken und voller Stolz den Vater als einen idealen Helden preist, und sie erzählt Hildebrand alles, was er wissen muss, um sich als Vater auszugeben. Zeugen, die den Alten vielleicht erkennen könnten, gibt es nicht, denn Hadubrand hat ja seine Kunde von Leuten, die alle tot sind, «dea erhina warun». Und diese Zeugen hatten ihm erzählt, dass der Name

seines Vaters Hildebrand war. Das war ist zu beachten.
Hier haben wir sofort, und ganz nebenbei, einen Hinweis
auf die felsenfeste Ueberzeugung des Sohnes, der Vater
sei tot. Darauf folgt wohin, warum und mit wem der
Vater seinerzeit floh. So, wie der Text dasteht, kann man
«enti sinero degano filu» nur auf Dietrich beziehen, was,
wie schon erwähnt, seine heldengeschichtlichen Schwie-
rigkeiten hat. Es wäre viel besser, wenn diese Krieger zu
Odoaker gehörten, obwohl eine solche Deutung etwas
gezwungen erscheinen mag. Beim Vortrag liesse sich die
Rückbeziehung von «sinero» auf Odoaker durch [37/38]
Tonfall andeuten. Unter anderem würde eine solche
Auffassung uns erklären, warum Dietrich so «friuntlaos»
war. Darauf hören wir von der jungen Frau und dem
jungen Kind und dem Elend, in dem der Vater sie
zurückliess. Das Kind ist «barn unwahsan», und das sollte
eigentlich nur bedeuten können: jung, unerwachsen. In
den anderen drei Versionen ist das Kind ein nachge-
borener Sohn. Nach Kap. 368 der *Þiðrekssaga* verliess
Hildebrand die Mutter vor der Geburt des Sohnes. Auf
dieses späte Zeugnis ist wenig Verlass. Schon Wilhelm
Grimm erwog, ob «unwahsan» nicht ungeboren
bedeuten könnte. Poetischer wäre es sicher, wenn die zwei
sich nie gesehen hätten. Das Wort scheint im Althoch-
deutschen sonst nicht belegt zu sein. Im Altenglischen
haben wir eine Reihe von Beispielen, immer im Sinne
von unerwachsen. Auch lässt sich nicht behaupten,
dass man «brut» nicht von einer jungen Mutter sagen
kann, denn in der *Alts. Genesis* 332 heisst die Frau von
Lot «brud», und zwar nicht im Stabreim, sodass der
Dichter ebensogut hätte «fri» oder «idis» schreiben
können.

Die Rede endet mit dem stolzen Preis des kriegerischen,
draufgängerischen Vaters, der immer in der vordersten

Reihe kämpfte und der unter Helden hochberühmt war. «Es ist kaum anzunehmen, dass er noch lebt» ist höflich, doch kann es in diesem Zusammenhang nur bedeuten «er ist tot». Immerhin, ein Funke von Zweifel an dem Tode ist doch, wenn man will, in diese Worte hineinzuhören, und so hat es der Dichter gewollt. Es gibt dem Zuhörer eine leise Hoffnung, alles möge sich zum Guten wenden, und auch für den Vater ist es eine Ermutigung.

Biz zu diesem Augenblick ist der Jüngere höflich und zuvorkommend. Er hat dem Aelteren alles Nötige mitgeteilt, und dieser ist nicht in der Lage, irgend einen neuen Beweis zu erbringen. Ein Zeichen hat er nicht, die Zeugen sind alle tot. Er, der Fremde, Unbekannte, kann nur sein Wort geben. Gewöhnlich wird angenommen, dass hier eine Lücke fällt zwischen der Rede des Sohnes und der des Vaters. Gewiss stimmt etwas nicht mit der letzten dem Sohne zugeschrieben Zeile: «ni waniu ih iu lib habbe». Der Stabreim fehlt. Viel kann jedoch [38/39] nicht ausgefallen sein. Die Rede endet mit der höflich ausgesprochenen Meinung vom Tode des Vaters.

So, wie die Antwort Hildebrands überliefert ist, ist sie kurz. Auch ist sie, was die Einzelheiten betrifft, dunkel. Wie man das erste, jetzt nicht mehr lesbare Wort wettu — wenn dies wirklich in der Handschrift stand — zu erklären hat, über diese Frage gibt es eine stattliche völlig nutzlose Literatur. Wichtiger ist das nächste Wort «irmingot», und das ist klar zu lesen. In der folgenden Zeil fehlt wiederum die Alliteration, und dann folgt eine vereinzelte Halbzeile. Trotz der fehlerhaften Ueberlieferung ist der Sinn deutlich genug. Keiner auf Erden kann dem Alten helfen. Der grosse Gott soll sein Zeuge sein, der Christengott, denn Dichter und Zuhörer sind Christen. In dem Lied ist nichts Heidnisches. Ein tapferer Kämpfer, der sich knirschend mit einem feindlichen

Schicksal abfindet, braucht kein Heide zu sein. Aber, wie gewöhnlich unter solchen Umständen: Gott schweigt. «Niemals, und das kann Gott bezeugen, hast du mit einem dir so nah verwandten Manne zu tun gehabt». Man meint häufig, jetzt müsse Hildebrand beteuert haben, er sei der lang vermisste Vater. Warum? Hadubrand hat offensichtlich keine anderen männlichen Verwandten; in diesem Zusammenhang kann «sus sippan man» daher nur bedeuten: «Ich bin dein Vater». Dieser Erklärung folgt auf dem Fusse das Angebot goldenen Schmucks als Zeichen des guten Willens.

Dies ist genug und übergenug für den bislang höflichen Hadubrand. Er ist zum Kampfe angetreten, er hat nicht den geringsten Grund, dem alten Manne zu trauen, die Anrufung Gottes muss ihm wie Gotteslästerung erscheinen, und er fürchtet irgend eine Kriegslist. Seine zweite Rede ist daher eine geschliffene Absage. «Feindesgaben sollen auf der Speerspitze dargeboten werden. Du bist ein sehr verschlagener alter Hunne. Während du schönredest, suchst du nach einer Gelegenheit, mich mit deinem Speere zu treffen. Deine List hat dich so lange am Leben erhalten, nicht dein Mut».

Hier werden die Zeilen 46–48, die in der Handschrift Hildebrand zugeschrieben sind, wahrscheinlich hingehören. «An deiner Ausrüstung ersehe ich, dass du daheim einen dir wohlge- [39/40] sinnten Herrn hast, und dass du von diesem Reiche nie vertrieben worden bist». Im Munde Hildebrands sind die Zeilen schwer verständlich, Hadubrand können wir sie ohne irgendwelche Schwierigkeit zuschreiben. Dass man sich mit den Zeilen, so wie sie dastehen, abfinden kann, ist damit nicht gesagt. Die erste liest sich wie Prosa und ihr fehlt der Stabreim, die dritte reimt «riche»: «reccheo», ein Reim, der im Bairischen vor 750 kaum möglich war. Trotzdem fühlt man: hier steckt etwas Altes, das verschüttet und verschleppt worden ist. Im Munde des Jungen ist es die verächtliche und wohlgezielte Antwort an den herrlich Ausgerüsteten, der goldene Ringe zu verschenken hat. So sieht ein Verbannter und Vertriebener wahrhaftig nicht aus! Und darauf folgt dann, klipp und klar, der für Hadubrand positive Beweis, dass Hildebrand lügt und auf Trug sinnt: «Seefahrer, die nach Westen über das Mittelmeer fuhren, berichteten mir, dass der Krieg ihn hinwegraffte. Hildebrand, der Sohn Heribrands, ist tot». Ebenso wie die erste Rede Hadubrands mit der Erwähnung des Todes des Vaters endet, obwohl höflich vorgebracht, so endet auch die zweite Rede mit dem Tode des Vaters. Jetzt jedoch werden Seefahrer als Zeugen angeführt und der Tod wird als eine harte, unumstössliche Gewissheit hingestellt. Man fühlt, dass hier alles Reden vergebens sein wird und dass sich der tragische Knoten schürzt.

Es besteht daher durchaus kein Grund, noch eine weitere Lücke anzunehmen. Die nächste Rede Hildebrands beginnt wiederum mit einer Anrufung Gottes. In der ersten sollte die Anrufung Gottes die Wahrheit beteuern, in der zweiten vernehmen wir den verzweifelten Aufschrei des gemarterten Vaters, dem der waltende Gott auch nicht helfen kann. «Weh! nun, allmächtiger Gott, ein entsetzliches Schicksal dräut» schliesst sich erbarmungslos und folgerecht an «Tot ist Hildebrand, der Sohn Heribrands» an. Die beiden Aussagen, als Höhepunkt der Handlung, gehören zusammen, und die Bühnenanweisung Zeile 45: «Hildebrand sprach, der Sohn Heribrands», kann man mit gutem Gewissen streichen. Es folgt die elegische Klage des [40/41] Vaters, der dreissig Jahre lang in Streit und Sturm dem Tod entgangen ist nur, um schliesslich in einem Kampf sich verwickelt zu sehen, wo Vater und Sohn sich auf Leben und Tod gegenüberstehen. Dann rafft er sich zusammen, der Krieger in ihm erwacht. «Der sei doch der feigste der Ostleute, der dich jetzt vom Kampfe abzuhalten sucht». Bei dem Wort für feig — «argosto» — hat man gemeint, Hadubrand müsse Hildebrand dieses Schimpfwort arg zugeschleudert haben. Wieder eine Lücke? Hadubrands zweite Rede ist verächtlich und beleidigend genug. Wir kommen auch ohne Lücke gut aus.

Der Kampf beginnt und schon nach fünfeinhalb Zeilen sind die Speere verschossen und im Nahkampf die Schilde zerhauen. Der Dichter verschwendet nicht allzuviel Zeit auf die blossen technischen Einzelheiten des Kampfes. Und an dieser Stelle bricht das Fragment ab. Dass der Sohn sterben musste, und der Vater ihn überlebte, nachdem er sein eigenes Geschlecht zerstört hatte, können wir zwar nicht beweisen, aber so muss es nach der ganzen Anlage gewesen sein. Auch haben wir das nordische Zeugnis der *Asmundarsaga kappabana* aus dem 14. Jahrhundert, in dem ein sterbender Held Hildebrand, von seinem Halbbruder Asmund hingestreckt, seinen Schild beschreibt, auf dem 80 Helden dargestellt sind, die vor seiner Klinge geblieben sind. Einer von ihnen ist sein eigner Sohn, «enn svasi sonr»; das «suasat chind» des *Hildebrandsliedes* zeigt, woher die nordische Kunde stammen muss. Die anderen Versionen helfen nicht weiter. Unser Dichter ist so unabhängig und so selbständig in der Erfindung poetischer Motive und Zusammenhänge, dass es müssig ist, einen möglichen Schluss zurechtzuzimmern.

Als der Dichter sein Lied schuf, gab es schon Dichtung über Dietrich, seine Flucht aus seinem Erbland, oder vorsichtiger: das Verlassen seines Erblandes, sein dreissigjähriges Exil, grösstenteils am Hofe des Hunnenherrschers. Diese Dietrichdichtung kann erst entstanden

sein eine geraume Weile nach dem Tode des geschicht-
lichen Theoderich im Jahre 526. Dreissig bis vierzig Jahre
ist wohl das geringste, das wir annehmen können, und
es muss sich hier um Heldendichtung handeln, vor einem
Fürsten und seinem Gefolge in der Halle vorgetragen.
Das Gotenreich [41/42] in Italien ging aber schon zu
dieser Zeit unter. In den fünfziger Jahren des 6. Jahr-
hunderts muss es noch manchen gotischen Adligen
gegeben haben, dem es nicht im Traum eingefallen wäre,
Dietrich mit Attila zu verbinden oder gar die tolle
Geschichtsfälschung ruhig hinzunehmen.

Kaum 40 Jahre nach dem Tode Dietrichs rückten die
Langobarden in Italien ein und übernahmen das gotische
Reich und Erbe. Gab es zu der Zeit schon Heldendichtung
von Dietrich? Erinnerungen, Erzählungen, Anekdoten
von dem grossen König wird es gegeben haben. Diese
wurden an die Langobarden vermittelt, bei denen die
geschichtliche Wahrheit dann auf den Kopf gestellt
wurde, sicher unter Mitwirkung von Goten. Wie viel von
diesem Dietrichmaterial etwas später in Heldenliedform
an langobardischen Höfen erklang, bleibt Vermutung. Es
ist nicht einzusehen, warum wir nicht annehmen sollten,
die Langobarden hätten sich die Ueberlieferungen ihrer
Vorgänger angeeignet und sie dann in Liedform ver-
breitet. Kurz und gut: setzen wir Dietrichdichtungen vor
550 an gotischen Höfen an, so können wir nicht begreifen,
wie die gewaltigen Umbiegungen der Geschichte so rasch
zustandegekommen sind. Setzen wir sie etwas später an
und als langobardische, von gotischen Traditionen
beeinflusste Lieder, wird die Ueberlieferung verständ-
licher.

Die Langobarden gaben diese Lieder an den Norden
weiter, an die freundnachbarlichen Bayern, mit denen sie
über 200 Jahre lang treue Freundschaft wahrten, von

anderen Erwägungen ganz abgesehen, schon der im Westen drohenden Franken wegen, die schliesslich sowohl Bayern wie Langobarden überrannten. Die in Italien lebenden Germanen wurden romanisiert. Ihre germanische Dichtung ging unter. Bei den Bayern hielt sie sich bis tief in das Mittelalter hinein. Man hat an versprengte Goten gedacht, die gotische Sage nach Oberdeutschland brachten. Es handelt sich aber zu dieser Zeit um Heldendichtung, die von Hof zu Hof wandert. Es bleibt einfacher, langobardische dichterische Vermittlung anzunehmen.

Beim *Hildebrandslied* selbst sehen wir etwas klarer. Wie schon Heusler vermutete, führen die *-brand* Namen uns zu den [42/43] Langobarden. Bei ihnen gab es eine reiche dichterische Ueberlieferung, die wir aus Paulus Diaconus und anderen Quellen erschliessen können. König Alboin, im Jahre 572 ermordet, ist der letzte südgermanische Held, der in der heroischen Dichtung eine Rolle spielt. Dass er überall besungen wurde, bezeugen Paulus Diaconus und der *Widsith*. Seit Heusler ist manches hinzugekommen und an dem langobardischen Ursprung ist nicht mehr zu zweifeln, obschon uns diese Einsicht nicht berechtigt, nun auch langobardische Urtexte zu fabrizieren.

Die geographischen Einzelheiten fügen sich gut ein. In Italien, zur Ostgotenzeit, war an der Ostgrenze einigermassen Ruhe. Unter den Langobarden wurde dies anders. Sie hatten einen schweren Stand gegen Avaren und mit ihnen verbündete Stämme, die immer wieder versuchten, von der pannonischen Tiefebene aus über die Friauler Landschaft nach Italien durchzustossen. Wenn wir annehmen, die beiden Heere liegen irgendwo nördlich einer Linie von Verona nach Ravenna, von Bern nach Raben, können wir verstehen, wieso Hadubrand Nachricht erhält vom Tode des Vaters von Seefahrern, die westlich über das adriatische Meer segeln. Solche überzeugend richtigen geographischen Einzelheiten müssen schon von dem ersten Dichter stammen, der die Gegend kennt. Sie erscheinen nebenbei im Gedicht, sie passen zu allem, was wir von Bern und Raben wissen, und sie waren auch den Zuhörern vertraut.

Und das Datum: das Gedicht mag wenig nach 600 an einem langobardischen Hofe vorgetragen worden sein. Später kam es zu den nördlichen Grenznachbarn, den Bayern. In Oberdeutschland wurde 'der alte Waffenmeister' fast ein Nationalheld, in England war er wahrscheinlich unbekannt. Wie er in die späte *Asmundarsaga kappabana* verpflanzt wurde, wissen wir nicht.

Ein langobardischer Dichter kennt die Fabel vom Vater-Sohnkampf, in dem der Sohn fällt, er kennt ursprünglich auf klassischem Boden beheimatete Geschichten, in denen ausgewählte Kempen statt der Heere kämpfen und in denen einer fallen muss. Diese beiden Fabeln verbindet er und baut sie in eine Geschichte der Heimkehr Dietrichs in sein rechtmässiges Königtum ein. Es war ein genialer Griff eines grossen Dichters, [43/44] diese beiden Fabeln zu verbinden, und trotz der kümmerlichen und trümmerhaften Ueberlieferung stehen die Helden in ihrem Stolz und in ihrer Not lebendig vor uns, und über die Jahrhunderte hinweg sehen wir das verstehende Lächeln des Dichters, tragisch und resigniert[1].

[Reprinted from Studi Germanici, Rivista dell' Istituto Italiano di studi germanici — Roma, Nuova serie, (1963), pp. 19–44.]

REFERENCES

¹ Auf Literaturhinweise und Belege ist hier verzichtet worden. Das altbe-
währte Braunesche Lesebuch (W. Braune – K. Helm, *Althochdeutsches Lesebuch*,
1959¹³), gibt in den Anmerkungen eine ausgezeichnete Bibliographie. Vgl. ferner
Siegfried Beyschlag, 'Hiltibrant enti Hadubrant untar heriun tuem', *Festgabe für
L. L. Hammerich*, Kopenhagen, 1962, SS. 13–28, wo die neusten Arbeiten z. T.
verzeichnet und berücksichtigt werden. Auf die gut fundierten Ausführungen
von Beyschlag, denen ich jedoch nicht überall beipflichten kann, komme ich an
anderer Stelle zurück. Zu vergleichen wäre ferner der ursprünglich in *Germanisch-
Romanische Monatsschrift* 34 (1953), SS. 257–74 und *Ogom* 9 (1957), jetzt mit einem
Nachwort erschienene Aufsatz von Jan de Vries, 'Das Motiv des Vater-Sohn
Kampfes im Hildebrandslied', SS. 248–84 [herausgegeben] von W. Hauck,
Zur Germanisch-Deutschen Heldensage, Darmstadt, 1961. Mit vielen der von de Vries
vorgebrachten Meinungen kann ich mich durchaus nicht befreunden, und ich
werde mich in einem weiteren Aufsatz des näheren mit seinen Ansichten
auseinandersetzen.

APPENDIX

[A letter from Andreas Heusler to Frederick Norman, thanking him for the gift of an offprint of 'Some problems of the *Hildebrandslied*', the first of the three essays reprinted above.]

Arlesheim bei Basel
  Haus Thule   1 Juni 1937

Wenn diese Zeilen Sie erreichen, hochgeehrter Herr, sollen sie Ihnen sagen, dasz ich grosze Freude hatte an Ihrem Hildebrandsaufsatz. Ich danke Ihnen, dasz Sie mir einen Abzug schickten, sonst wär ich auf immer drum gekommen.

Sie sind jedenfalls eine Rara avis unter den Hildebrandspezialisten, sofern Sie etwas Humor durchblitzen lassen!

Aus dem Herzen kommt mir, was Sie p. 6 ff. gegen die Nur-Linguisten sagen . . . und so manches andre.

Haben Sie einmal beachtet, wie viele der Emendationen einfach schon aus metrischem Grund ausscheiden? Der seligen Typentheorie muszte das Hildebr. als ein Wildling gelten. Zählt es doch keine Silben! Ergo fand man bei Konjekturen alles erlaubt. Aber dieser Vers, so frei er ist, hat seine Grundsätze, und Konjekturen wie 'du sîs chind' oder die schauerliche von E. A. Kock, p. 14 verdienen keine Erörterung. Ebenso wenig die fühllosen 'Schwellverse', die der selige Grienberger erzeugte.

Ich finde noch ein Expl. eines uralten Vortrages von mir und wage, es Ihnen als Zeichen meines Danks zu schicken. Kaum darf ich mir schmeicheln, der Vortrag werde Sie irre machen an Ihrem Satz, p. 22 'We cannot escape . . . the poet himself.' Ich möchte umgekehrt sagen: Die gründliche Umformung der prägermanischen Vater-Sohnfabel wird uns nur verständlich, wenn wir den treuen Waffenmeister als Figur des Dietrichlieds annehmen. Die Einwände Schneiders, p. 22, sind nicht wohl bedacht. 'Der Name stimmt nicht': gewisz, den einen hat der Langobarde geschaffen für séine Fabel, der andre war geschichtlich gotisch! 'Eine Fabel oder Rolle besteht nicht': das konnte Schneider nur schreiben, weil er sich drauf verbissen hatte, den Liedinhalt 'Dietrichs Flucht' zu leugnen. 'Die Funktion ist ganz typisch': typisch werden Dichtungsmotive erst dadurch, dasz mehr als éiner sie verwendet. Eben dies nehmen wir hier an; & Schneider leugnet es.

Schlagen Sie doch einmal, wenn es Ihnen zugänglich ist, das Buch Waldemar Haupts nach: Zur niederdt. Dietrichsage (1914). Darin ist die Antwort schon richtig erteilt, welche Rolle der treue Waffenmeister im Fluchtlied hatte, also der anfängliche *Gêsimund, der dann seinen Namen dem 'Hildebrand' der Langobarden opfern muszte. Auch sonst steht vieles in jenem Buch, das Schneider zu seinem Schaden nicht gewürdigt hat.

Noch ein Wort zu dem 'darba gistuontun'. Genügt denn nicht die summarische Vorstellung: Dtr hatte weiterhin den Hbr dringend nötig? Man *musz* da nicht an einzelne Lagen denken; deren bietet die mhd. Dichtg (+ Thidr.s.) mehrere. Ich bin dagegen, dasz man solche Anspielungen in scharfe Zitronenpresser tue.

... Noch éins: empfinden Sie nicht mit mir, dasz Hadubr.s Rückblick Z.18 ff. erst dann rechte Farbe & Wirkung gewinnt, wenn man sich ein Dietrichslied dazu ergänzen kann? — Mir *beweist* dieser Rückblick, dasz die Langobarden ein gotisches Fluchtlied kannten.

Aber ich werde geschwätzig . . . Haltens zugut

Ihrem sehr ergebenen

A. HEUSLER

[Typewritten]